Scorpio

Dedication

For the memory of Gary Bailey, a new star in heaven.
For the memory of Frances Waxman, who always marched to her own drum beat.

Acknowledgements

We gratefully acknowledge the help given to us by Lynn Beddoe, Claire Champion, Anne Christie, Grant Griffiths and Liz Dean who have all helped enormously with the production of this book.

Scorpio

Sasha Fenton and Jonathan Dee

This edition published 1996 for Parragon Books
Units 13–17 Avonbridge Industrial Estate
Atlantic Road
Avonmouth, Bristol BS11 9QD
by Diamond Books
77–85 Fulham Palace Road
Hammersmith, London W6 8JB

ISBN 0 75251 908 5

Phototypeset by Intype London Ltd
Printed in Great Britain

Contents

The Essential Scorpio

YOUR RULING PLANET Your ruling body is Pluto, the Roman god of the underworld. Pluto is associated with great wealth, most of which is hidden underground, as well as birth, death and sex. Before Pluto was discovered, Scorpio was assigned to Mars, the red planet, which is associated with the Roman god of war.

YOUR SYMBOL The scorpion is your symbol. The scorpion once made the mistake of stinging the giant, Orion, who threw him into the sky where he now exisits as far as away from Orion as is possible. The scorpion turns its sting on itself if it feels threatened. The ancient symbol for your sign used to be the eagle. This denotes the higher side of Scorpio, which can soar above everything that is base, coarse and petty.

PARTS OF THE BODY The sexual organs, the lower stomach, lower spine and groin. Also blood and eyes.

YOUR GOOD BITS You have great endurance, tenacity and self-control. Your willpower will overcome almost anything. You are very caring and protective towards your family, especially your partner.

YOUR BAD BITS You can be secretive, suspicious, inflexible, vindictive and ruthless.

YOUR WEAKNESSES Self-destruction, violence, moodiness, clannishness.

YOUR BEST DAY Tuesday. Tuesday is traditionally assigned to the Roman god, Mars.

YOUR WORST DAY Friday.

YOUR COLOURS Dark red, dark purple.

CITIES Milwaukee, Washington DC, New Orleans, Liverpool, Brisbane.

COUNTRIES Norway, Syria, Brazil, Zimbabwe.

HOLIDAYS You are too restless to sit about on a beach for long. A sea cruise probably appeals because you love the sea and you enjoy waking up in new places every day.

YOUR FAVOURITE CAR You need a big, fast, powerful automatic limo with tinted windows and plenty of gadgets in it. An ejector seat for irritating passengers would be nice.

YOUR FAVOURITE MEAL OUT Your stomach is sensitive, so spicy foods and anything that is unfamiliar is not liked. Many Scorpios enjoy eating soup, either the thin kind with a little pasta added or a thick country broth. Traditional astrology suggests peppers; we suggest that you hold the peppers and go for the leeks instead!

YOUR FAVOURITE DRINK Scorpios either drink a great deal or practically nothing at all. Many of you enjoy whisky, especially the many different kinds of malts.

YOUR HERB Basil.

YOUR TREES Blackthorn, hawthorn, or any thorny bush or tree, possibly something like acacia.

YOUR FLOWERS Rhododendron, dark red flowers, also cacti.

YOUR ANIMALS Scorpion, eagle, shark, mule and snake.

YOUR METAL Iron. This metal is associated with Mars,

the ancient ruler of Scorpio. Iron has a low melting point and it oxidises, or rusts, to a reddish colour. These days plutonium has been added as a Scorpio metal, but it isn't recommended to wear this as jewellery!

YOUR GEMS Opal, obsidian, onyx, jet, marcasite.

MODE OF DRESS You love to shock, so you could turn up looking like Cher in one of her more outrageous outfits. Otherwise, both sexes like wearing casual clothes such as jeans and colourful shirts.

YOUR CAREERS Police, forensic or medical work, especially surgery and psychiatry. Butcher, miner, engineer.

YOUR FRIENDS People who are not afraid of you and who are as passionate about life as you are.

YOUR ENEMIES Timid types or aloof, pretentious ones.

YOUR FAVOURITE GIFT You hate anything that is cheap and nasty so any gift, however small, should be of the highest quality. You love music so a couple of CDs or tickets to a musical or pop event would delight you. Nice clothes or something attractive for the home always goes down well, as does aftershave, perfume or good jewellery.

YOUR LUCKY NUMBER Your lucky number is 8. To find your lucky number on a raffle ticket or something similar, first add the number together. For example, if one of your lottery numbers is 28, add 2 + 8 to make 10; then add 1 + 0, to give the root number of 1. The number 316 on a raffle ticket works in the same way. Add 3 + 1 + 6 to make 10: then add 1 + 0, making 1. As any number that adds up to 8 is lucky for you, numbers 17, 161 or 314 would work. A selection of lottery numbers should include some of the following: 8, 17, 26, 35 or 44.

Your Sun Sign

Scorpio

Ruled by Pluto and Mars
24th October to 22nd November

Yours is a feminine, water sign whose symbol is the scorpion. The feminine, water aspect suggests that yours is a gentle and loving sign, yet Scorpios have a very bad press in all astrology books, being described as passionate, determined, hot-tempered, drunken, cruel and vengeful. The truth, as you shall see, is somewhere in between.

You have the greatest endurance of any sign of the zodiac. You can cope with a hard job, a difficult partner or a set of crushing circumstances better than most. You have great pride and very high personal standards and you would consider yourself spineless if you walked away from trouble. You are extremely loyal and very loving to those whom you are close to. You don't let your family down and you can even care for a cantankerous parent if necessary. However, you don't keep your feelings to yourself and, if you are being put upon, you let people know it. The one thing you really cannot take is being abandoned or betrayed by someone in whom you have placed your trust, and you don't forgive anyone who parts you from anything or anyone you consider to be yours.

Something in your childhood may have undermined your confidence. Your parents may have preferred another sister or brother to you, or you may have been made to feel inferior or insecure by schoolmates, or by the people whom you lived amongst. You could, alternatively, have been envied by others for being brighter than them. You are slow to trust others, and you don't let other people into the secrets of your bank account, your private life or your real feelings. Only those who love you know when all isn't well, because you don't allow others to see what you deem to be weakness or failure. Some of you feel that you are missing out on your share of money, love or other goodies. When a situation becomes intolerable, either in personal life or in a job, you can set about destroying it completely, cutting your own nose off to spite your face in the process. If you manage to find the right partner and the right boss, you are the soul of loyalty and you will do all that you can for them. You will support your partner in his or her career and you would sacrifice anything in order to push a talented child. This scenario does not fit all Scorpios because there are plenty of you who have happy childhoods and good relationships in adult life. However, you may be drawn to choose a difficult partner who presents a challenge.

Some of you are as sexy as your reputation says you are while others go through life being surprisingly innocent and inhibited. All of you enjoy being thought of as sexy and some of you enjoy making saucy remarks. You are honest, dependable, talented and, when you want to be, extremely charming. You probably have a wonderful speaking voice and a sharp intellect. People either love you dearly or fear you. You can be terribly afraid of life itself at times and you can worry yourself sick about practically anything, but you have the courage and endurance to overcome almost anything. You have the most wonderful recuperative powers and can overcome even death itself – for a while at least.

All the Other Sun Signs

Aries

21st March to 20th April

Ariens can get anything they want off the ground, but it may land back down again with a bump. They are quick to think and to act, often intelligent and with no patience for fools. This includes anyone who is slower than themselves.

They are not the tidiest of people and they are impatient with details, except when engaged upon their special subject: *then* Ariens can fiddle around for hours. They are willing to make huge financial sacrifices for their families and they can put up with relatives living with them as long as this leaves them free to do their own thing. Aries women are decisive and competitive at work but many are uninterested in homemaking. They might consider giving up a relationship if it interfered with their ambitions. Highly sexed and experimental, they are faithful while in love but, if love begins to fade, they start to look around. Ariens may tell themselves that they are only looking for amusement, but they may end up in a fulfilling relationship with someone else's partner. This kind of situation offers the continuity and emotional support which they need with no danger of boredom or entrapment.

Their faults are those of impatience and impetuosity, coupled with a hot temper. They can pick a furious row with a supposed adversary, tear him or her to pieces then walk away from the situation five minutes later, forgetting all about it. Unfortunately, the poor victim can't always shake off the effects of the row in quite the same way. However, Arien cheerfulness, spontaneous generosity and kindness make them the greatest friends to have.

Taurus

21st April to 21st May

These people are practical and persevering. Taureans are solid and reliable, regular in habits, sometimes a bit wet behind the ears and stubborn as mules. Their love of money and the comfort it can bring may make them very materialistic in outlook. They are most suited to a practical career which brings with it few surprises and plenty of money. However, they have a strong artistic streak which can be expressed in work, hobbies and interests.

Some Taureans are quick and clever, highly amusing and quite outrageous in appearance. But underneath this crazy exterior is a background of true talent and very hard work. This type may be a touch arrogant. Other Taureans hate to be rushed or hassled, preferring to work quietly and thoroughly at their own pace. These people take relationships very seriously and they make safe and reliable partners. They may keep their worries to themselves but they are not usually liars or sexually untrustworthy.

Being so very sensual as well as patient, these people make excellent lovers. Their biggest downfall comes later in life when they have a tendency to plonk themselves down in front of the television night after night and tune out the rest of the world. Another problem with some

Taureans is their 'pet hate'. This is something which has long since got under their skins and which they go on about at any given opportunity. Their virtues are common sense, loyalty, responsibility and a pleasant, non-hostile approach to others. Taureans are much brighter than anyone gives them credit, and it is hard to beat them in an argument because they usually know what they are talking about. If a Taurean is on your side, they make wonderful friends and comfortable and capable colleagues.

Gemini

22nd May to 21st June

Geminis are often accused of being short on intellect and unable to stick to anyone or anything for long. In short, great fun at a party but totally unreliable. This is unfair; nobody works harder, is more reliable or capable than Geminis when they put their mind to a task, especially if there is a chance of making large sums of money! Unfortunately, they have a low boredom threshold and they can drift away from something or someone when it no longer interests them. They like to be busy, with plenty of variety in their lives and the opportunity to communicate with others. Their forte is the communications industry where they shamelessly pinch ideas and improve on them. Many Geminis are highly ambitious people who won't allow anything or anyone to stand in their way.

They are surprisingly constant in relationships, often marrying for life but, if it doesn't work out, they will walk out and put the experience behind them. Geminis need relationships and if one fails, they will soon start looking for the next. Faithfulness is another story, because the famed Gemini curiosity can lead to any number of adventures. Geminis educate their children well while neglecting to see whether they have a clean shirt. The house is full of books, videos, televisions, CDs, newspapers and magazines and there is a phone in every room as well as in the car, the loo and the Gemini lady's handbag.

Cancer

22nd June to 23rd July

Cancerians look for security on the one hand and adventure and novelty on the other. They are popular because they really listen to what others are saying. Their own voices are attractive too. They are naturals for sales work and in any kind of advisory capacity. Where their own problems are concerned, they can disappear inside themselves and brood, which makes them hard for others to understand. Cancerians spend a good deal of time worrying about their families and, even more so, about money. They appear soft but are very hard to influence.

Many Cancerians are small traders and many more work in teaching or the caring professions. They have a feel for history and may collect historical mementoes and their memory is excellent. They need to have a home but they love to travel away from it, being happy in the knowledge that it is there waiting for them to come back to. There are a few Cancerians who seem to drift through life and expect other members of their family to keep them.

Romantically, they prefer to be settled and they fear being alone. A marriage would need to be really bad before they left, and if they do, they soon look for a new partner. These people can be scoundrels in business because they hate parting with money once they have their hands on it. However, their charm and intelligence usually manage to get them out of trouble.

Leo

24th July to 23rd August

Leos can be marvellous company or a complete pain in the neck. Under normal circumstances, they are warm-hearted, generous, sociable and popular but they can be very moody and irritable when under pressure or under the weather. Leos put their heart and soul in to whatever they are doing and they can work like demons for a while. However, they cannot keep up the pace for long and they need to get away, zonk out on the sofa and have frequent holidays. These people always appear confident and they look like the true winners, but their confidence can suddenly evaporate, leaving them unsure and unhappy with their efforts. They are extremely sensitive to hurt and they cannot take ridicule or even very much teasing.

Leos are proud. They have very high standards in all that they do and most have great integrity and honesty, but there are some who are complete and utter crooks. These people can stand on their dignity and be very snobbish. Their arrogance can become insufferable and they can take their powers of leadership into the realms of bossiness. They are convinced that they should be in charge and they can be very obstinate. They love the status and lifestyle which proclaims their successes. Many Leos work in glamour professions such as the airline or the entertainment industries. Others spend their day communing with computers and other high-tech gadgetry. In loving relationships, they are loyal but only while the magic lasts. If boredom sets in, they can start looking around for fresh fields. They are the most generous and loving of people and they need to play affectionately. Leos are kind, charming and they live life to the full.

Virgo

24th August to 23rd September

Virgos are highly intelligent, interested in everything and everyone and happy to be busy with many jobs and hobbies. Many have some kind of specialised knowledge and most are good with their hands. Their nit-picking ways can infuriate their colleagues. They find it hard to discuss their innermost feelings and this can make them hard to understand. In many ways, they are happier doing something practical than dealing with relationships. These people can overdo the self-sacrificial bit and make themselves martyrs to other people's impractical lifestyles. They are willing to fit in with whatever is going on and they can adjust to most things, but they mustn't neglect their own needs.

Although excellent communicators and wonderfully witty conversationalists, Virgos prefer to express their deepest feelings by actions rather than words. Most avoid touching all but very close friends and family members and they find lovey-dovey behaviour embarrassing. These people can be very highly sexed and they may use this as a way of expressing love. Virgos are criticised a good deal as children and often made to feel unwelcome in their childhood homes. They in turn become very critical of others and they can use this in order to wound. Many Virgos overcome inhibitions by taking up acting, music, cookery or sports.

Acting is particularly common to this sign because it allows them to put aside their fears and take on the mantle of someone quite different. They are shy and slow to make friends but when they do accept someone, they are the loyalest, gentlest and kindest of companions. They are great company and have a wonderful sense of humour.

Libra

24th September to 23rd October

Librans have a deceptive appearance, looking soft but being tough and quite selfish underneath. Astrological tradition tells us that this sign is dedicated to marriage but a high proportion of them prefer to remain single, particularly when a difficult relationship comes to an end. These people are great to tell secrets to because they never listen to anything properly and promptly forget whatever was said. The confusion between their desire to co-operate with others and the need for self-expression is even more evident when at work. The best job is one where they are a part of an organisation but are able to make their own decisions.

While some Librans are shy and lacking in confidence, others are strong and determined with definite leadership qualities. All need to find a job which entails dealing with others and which does not wear out their delicate nerves. All Librans are charming, sophisticated and diplomatic, but can be confusing to others.

All have a strong sense of justice and fair play but most haven't the strength to take on a determinedly lame duck. They project an image which is attractive, chosen to represent their sense of status and refinement. Being inclined to experiment sexually, they are not the most faithful of partners and even goody-goody Librans are terrible flirts.

Sagittarius

23rd November to 21st December

Sagittarians are great company because they are interested in everything and everyone. Broad-minded and lacking in prejudice, they are fascinated by even the strangest of people. With their optimism and humour, they are often the life and soul of the party, while they are in a good mood. They can become quite down-hearted, crabby and awkward on occasion, but not usually for long. They can be hurtful to others because they cannot resist speaking what they see as the truth, even if it causes embarrassment. However, their tactlessness is usually innocent and they have no desire to hurt.

Sagittarians need an unconventional lifestyle, preferably one which allows them to travel. They cannot be cooped up in a cramped environment and they need to meet new people and to explore a variety of ideas during their day's work. Money is not their god – they will work for a pittance if they feel inspired by the task. Their values are spiritual rather than material. Many are attracted to the spiritual side of life and may be interested in the Church, philosophy, astrology and other New Age subjects. Higher education and legal matters attract them because these subjects expand and explore intellectual boundaries. Long-lived relationships may not appeal because they need to feel free and unfettered, but they can do well with a self-sufficient and independent partner. Despite all this intellectualism and need for freedom, Sagittarians have a deep need to be cuddled and touched and they need to be supported emotionally.

Capricorn

22nd December to 20th January

Capricorns are patient, realistic and responsible and they take life seriously. They need security but they may find this difficult to achieve. Many live on a treadmill of work, simply to pay the bills and feed the kids. They take their family responsibilities seriously, even caring for distant relatives if this becomes necessary. However, they can play the martyr while doing so. These people hate coarseness, they are easily embarrassed and they hate to annoy anyone. They believe fervently in keeping the peace in their families. This doesn't mean that they cannot stand up for themselves, indeed they know how to get their own way and they won't be bullied. They are adept at using charm to get around prickly people.

Capricorns are ambitious, hard working, patient and status-conscious and they will work their way steadily towards the top in any organisation. If they run their own businesses, they need a partner with more pizazz to deal with sales and marketing for them while they keep an eye on the books. Their nit-picking habits can infuriate others and some have a tendency to 'know best' and not to listen. These people work at their hobbies with the same kind of dedication that they put into everything else. They are faithful and reliable in relationships and it takes a great deal to make them stray. If a relationship breaks up, they take a long time to get over it. They may marry very early or delay it until middle age when they are less shy. As an earth sign, Capricorns are highly sexed but they need to be in a relationship where they can relax and gain confidence. Their best attribute is their genuine kindness and their wonderfully dry, witty sense of humour.

Aquarius

21st January to 19th February

Clever, friendly, kind and humane, Aquarians are the easiest people to make friends with but probably the hardest to really know. They are often more comfortable with friends than with those who are close to them. Being dutiful, they would never let a member of their family go without their basic requirements, but they can be strangely, even deliberately, blind to their underlying needs and real feelings. They are more comfortable with causes and their idealistic ideas than with the day-to-day routine of family life. Their homes may reflect this lack of interest by being rather messy, although there are other Aquarians who are almost clinically house proud.

Their opinions are formed early in life and are firmly fixed. Being patient with people, they make good teachers and are, themselves, always willing to learn something new. But are they willing to go out and earn a living? Some are, many are not. These people can be extremely eccentric in the way they dress or the way they live. They make a point of being 'different' and they can actually feel very unsettled and uneasy if made to conform, even outwardly. Their restless, sceptical minds mean that they need an alternative kind of lifestyle which stretches them mentally.

In relationships, they are surprisingly constant and faithful and they only stray when they know in their hearts that there is no longer anything to be gained from staying put. Aquarians are often very attached to the first real commitment in their lives and they can even re-marry a previously divorced partner. Their sexuality fluctuates, peaking for some years then, perhaps, pushed aside while something else occupies their energies, then high again. Many Aquarians are extremely highly sexed and very clever and active in bed.

Pisces

20th February to 20th March

This idealistic, dreamy, kind and impractical sign needs a lot of understanding. They have a fractured personality which has so many sides and so many moods that they probably don't even understand themselves. Nobody is more kind, thoughtful and caring, but they have a tendency to drift away from people and responsibilities. When the going gets rough, they get going! Being creative, clever and resourceful, these people can achieve a great deal and really reach the top, but few of them do. Some Pisceans have a self-destruct button which they press before reaching their goal. Others do achieve success and the motivating force behind this essentially spiritual and mystical sign is often money. Many Pisceans feel insecure, most suffer some experience of poverty at some time in their early lives and they grow into adulthood determined that they will never feel that kind of uncertainty again.

Pisceans are at home in any kind of creative or caring career. Many can be found in teaching, nursing and the arts. Some find life hard and are often unhappy; many have to make tremendous sacrifices on behalf of others. This may be a pattern which repeats itself from childhood, where the message is that the Piscean's needs always come last. These people can be stubborn, awkward, selfish and quite nasty when a friendship or relationship goes sour. This is because, despite their basically kind and gentle personality, there is a side which needs to be in charge of any relationship. Pisceans make extremely faithful partners as long as the romance doesn't evaporate and their partners treat them well. Problems occur if they are mistreated or rejected, if they become bored or restless of if their alcohol intake climbs over the danger level. These people are sexual fantasists so in this sphere of life, anything can happen!

You and Yours

What is it like to bring up an Arien child? What kind of father does a Libran make? How does it feel to grow up with a Scorpio mother? Whatever your own sign is, how do you appear to your parents and how do you behave towards your children?

The Scorpio Father

These fathers can be really awful or absolutely wonderful, and there aren't any half-measures. Good Scorpio men provide love and security because they stick closely to their homes and families and are unlikely to do a disappearing act. Difficult ones can be loud and tyrannical. These proud men want their children to be the best and become so.

The Scorpio Mother

These mothers are either wonderful or not really maternal at all, although they try to do their best. If they take to child rearing, they encourage their offspring educationally and in their hobbies. These mothers have no time for whiny or miserable children but they respect outgoing, talented and courageous ones and they can cope with a handful.

The Scorpio Child

Scorpio children are competitive, self-centred and unwilling to co-operate with brothers, sisters, teachers or anyone else when in an awkward mood. They can be deeply unreadable living in a world of their own and filled with all kinds of strange angry feelings. At other times, they can be delightfully caring companions. They love animals, sports, children's organisations and group activities.

The Aries Father

Arien men take the duties of fatherhood very seriously. They read to their children, take them on educational trips and expose them to art and music from an early age. They can push their children too hard or tyrannise the sensitive ones. The Aries father wants his children not only to *have* what he didn't have but also to *be* what he isn't. He respects those children who are high achievers and who can stand up to him.

The Aries Mother

Arien women love their children dearly and will make amazing sacrifices for them, but don't expect them to give up their jobs or their outside interests for motherhood. Competitive herself, this mother wants her children to be the best and she may push them too hard. However, she is kind hearted, affectionate and not likely to over discipline them. She treats her offspring as adults and is well loved in return.

The Aries Child

Arien children are hard to ignore. Lively, noisy and demanding, they try to enjoy every moment of their childhood. Despite this, they lack confidence and need reassurance. Often clever but lacking in self-discipline, they need to be made to attend school each day and to do their homework. Active and competitive, these children excel in sports, dancing or learning to play a pop music instrument.

The Taurus Father

This man cares deeply for his children and wants the best for them, but he doesn't expect the impossible. He may lay the law down and he can be unsympathetic to the attitudes and interests of a new generation. He may frighten young children by shouting at them. Being a responsible parent, he offers a secure family base but he may find it hard to let them go when they want to leave.

The Taurus Mother

These women make good mothers due to their highly domesticated nature. Some are real earth mothers, baking bread and making wonderful toys and games for their children. Sane and sensible but not highly imaginative, they do best with a child who has ordinary needs and they get confused by those who are 'special' in any way. Taurus mothers are very loving but they use reasonable discipline when necessary.

The Taurus Child

Taurean children can be surprisingly demanding. Their loud voices and stubborn natures can be irritating. Plump, sturdy and strong, some are shy and retiring, while others can bully weaker children. Artistic, sensual, often musical; these children can lose themselves in creative or beautiful hobbies. They need to be encouraged to share and express love and also to avoid too many sweet foods.

The Gemini Father

Gemini fathers are fairly laid back in their approach and, while they cope well with fatherhood, they can become bored with home life and try to escape from their duties. Some are so absorbed with work that they hardly see their offspring. At home, Gemini fathers will provide books, educational toys and as much computer equipment as the child can use, and they enjoy a family game of tennis.

The Gemini Mother

These mothers can be very pushy because they see education as the road to success. She encourages a child to pursue any interest and will sacrifice time and money for this. They usually have a job outside the home and may rely on other people to do some child minding for them. Their children cannot always count on coming home to a balanced meal, but they can talk to their mothers on any subject.

The Gemini Child

These children needs a lot of reassurance because they often feel like square pegs in round holes. They either do very well at school and incur the wrath of less able children, or they fail dismally and have to make it up later in life. They learn to read early and some have excellent mechanical ability while others excel at sports. They get bored very easily and they can be extremely irritating.

The Cancer Father

A true family man who will happily embrace even step-children as if they were his own. Letting go of the family when they grow up is another matter. Cancerian sulks, moodiness and bouts of childishness can confuse or frighten some children, while his changeable attitude to money can make them unsure of what they should ask for. This father enjoys home making and child rearing and he may be happy to swap roles.

The Cancer Mother

Cancerian women are excellent homemakers and cheerful and reasonable mothers, as long as they have a part time job or an interest outside the house. They instinctively know when a child is unhappy and can deal with it in a manner which is both efficient and loving. These women have a reputation for clinging but most are quite realistic when the time comes for their brood to leave the nest.

The Cancer Child

These children are shy, cautious and slow to grow up. They may achieve little at school, 'disappearing' behind louder and more demanding classmates. They can be worriers who complain about every ache and pain or suffer from imaginary fears. They may take on the mother's role in the family, dictating to their sisters and brothers at times. Gentle and loving but moody and secretive, they need a lot of love and encouragement.

The Leo Father

These men can be wonderful fathers as long as they remember that children are not simply small and rather obstreperous adults. Leo fathers like to be involved with their children and encourage them to do well at school. They happily make sacrifices for their children and they truly want them to have the best, but they can be a bit too strict and they may demand too high a standard.

The Leo Mother

Leo mothers are very caring and responsible but they cannot be satisfied with a life of pure domesticity, and need to combine motherhood with a job. These mothers don't fuss about minor details. They're prepared to put up with a certain amount of noise and disruption, but they can be irritable and they may demand too much of their children.

The Leo Child

These children know almost from the day they are born that they are special. They are usually loved and wanted but they are also aware that a lot is expected from them. Leo children appear outgoing but they are surprisingly sensitive and easily hurt. They only seem to wake up to the need to study a day or so after they leave school, but they find a way to make a success of their lives.

The Virgo Father

These men may be embarrassed by open declarations of love and affection and find it hard to give cuddles and reassurance to small children. Yet they love their offspring dearly and will go to any lengths to see that they have the best possible education and outside activities. Virgoan men can become wrapped up in their work, forgetting to spend time relaxing and playing with their children.

The Virgo Mother

Virgoan women try hard to be good mothers because they probably had a poor childhood themselves. They love their children very much and want the best for them but they may be fussy about unnecessary details such as dirt on the kitchen floor or the state of the children's school books. If they can keep their tensions and longings away from their children, they can be the most kindly and loving parents.

The Virgo Child

Virgoan children are practical and capable and can do very well at school, but they are not always happy. They don't always fit in and they may have difficulty making friends. They may be shy, modest and sensitive and they can find it hard to live up to their own impossibly high standards. Virgo children don't need harsh discipline, they want approval and will usually respond perfectly well to reasoned argument.

The Libra Father

Libran men mean well, but they may not actually perform that well. They have no great desire to be fathers but welcome their children when they come along. They may slide out of the more irksome tasks by having an absorbing job or a series of equally absorbing hobbies which keep them occupied outside the home. These men do better with older children because they can talk to them.

The Libra Mother

Libran mothers are pleasant and easy going but some of them are more interested in their looks, their furnishings and their friends than their children. Others are very loving and kind but a bit too soft, which results in their children disrespecting them or walking all over them later in life. These mothers enjoy talking to their children and encouraging them to succeed.

The Libra Child

These children are charming and attractive and they have no difficulty in getting on with people. They make just enough effort to get through school and only do the household jobs they cannot dodge. They may drive their parents mad with their demands for the latest gadget or gimmick. However, their common sense, sense of humour and reasonable attitude makes harsh discipline unnecessary.

The Sagittarius Father

Sagittarian fathers will give their children all the education they can stand. They happily provide books, equipment and take their offspring out to see anything interesting. They may not always be available to their offspring, but they make up for it by surprising their family with tickets for sporting events or by bringing home a baby rabbit. These men are cheerful and childlike themselves.

The Sagittarius Mother

This mother is kind, easy going and pleasant. She may be very ordinary with suburban standards or she may be unbelievably eccentric, forcing the family to take up strange diets and filling the house with weird and wonderful people. Some opt out of child rearing by finding child minders while others take on other people's children and a host of animals in addition to their own.

The Sagittarius Child

Sagittarian children love animals and the outdoor life but they are just as interested in sitting around and watching the telly as the next child. These children have plenty of friends whom they rush out and visit at every opportunity. Happy and optimistic but highly independent, they cannot be pushed in any direction. Many leave home in late teens in order to travel.

The Capricorn Father

These are true family men who cope with housework and child rearing but they are sometimes too involved in work to spend much time at home. Dutiful and caring, these men are unlikely to run off with a bimbo or to leave their family wanting. However, they can be stuffy or out of touch with the younger generation. They encourage their children to do well and to behave properly.

The Capricorn Mother

Capricorn women make good mothers but they may be inclined to fuss. Being ambitious, they want their children to do well and they teach them to respect teachers, youth leaders and so on. These mothers usually find work outside the home in order to supplement the family income. They are very loving but they can be too keen on discipline and the careful management of pocket money.

The Capricorn Child

Capricorn children are little adults from the day they are born. They don't need much discipline or encouragement to do well at school. Modest and well behaved, they are almost too good to be true. However, they suffer badly with their nerves and can suffer from ailments like asthma. They need to be taught to let go, have fun and enjoy their childhood. Some are too selfish or ambitious to make friends.

The Aquarian Father

Some Aquarian men have no great desire to be fathers but they make a reasonable job of it when they have to. They cope best when their children are reasonable and intelligent but, if they are not, they tune out and ignore them. Some Aquarians will spend hours inventing games and toys for their children while all of them value education and try to push their children.

The Aquarian Mother

Some of these mothers are too busy putting the world to rights to see what is going on in their own family. However, they are kind, reasonable and keen on education. They may be busy outside the house but they often take their children along with them. Not being fussy homemakers, they are happy to have all the neighbourhood kids in the house. They respect a child's dignity.

The Aquarian Child

These children may be demanding when very young but they become much more reasonable when at school. They are easily bored and need outside interests. They have many friends and may spend more time in other people's homes than in their own. Very stubborn and determined, they make it quite clear from an early age that they intend to do things their own way. These children suffer from nerves.

The Pisces Father

Piscean men fall into one of two categories. Some are kind and gentle, happy to take their children on outings and to introduce them to art, culture, music or sport. Others are disorganised and unpredictable. The kindly fathers don't always push their children. They encourage their kids to have friends and a pet or two.

The Pisces Mother

Piscean mothers may be lax and absent minded but they love their children and are usually loved in return. Many are too disorganised to run a perfect household so meals, laundry etc. can be hit and miss, but their children prosper despite this, although many learn to reverse the mother/child roles. These mothers teach their offspring to appreciate animals and the environment.

The Pisces Child

These sensitive children may find life difficult and they can get lost among stronger, more demanding brothers and sisters. They may drive their parents batty by their dreamy attitude and they can make a fuss over nothing. They need a secure and loving home with parents who shield them from harsh reality while encouraging them to develop their imaginative and psychic abilities.

Your Rising Sign

What is a Rising Sign?

Your rising sign is the sign of the zodiac which was climbing up over the eastern horizon the moment you were born. This is not the same as your Sun sign; your Sun sign depends upon your date of birth, but your rising sign depends upon the time of day that you were born, combined with your date and place of birth.

The rising sign modifies your Sun sign character quite considerably, so when you have worked out which is your rising sign, read page 35 to see how it modifies your Sun sign. Then take a deeper look by going back to 'All the Other Sun Signs' on page 7 and read the relevant Sun sign material there to discover more about your ascendant (rising sign) nature.

Can Your Rising Sign Tell You More About Your Future?

When it comes to tracking events, the rising sign is equal in importance to the Sun sign. So, if you want a more accurate forecast when reading newspapers or magazines, you should read the horoscope for your rising sign as well as your Sun sign. In the case of books such as this, you should really treat yourself to two – one to correspond with your rising sign, and another for your usual Sun sign, and read both each day!

One final point is that the sign that is opposite your rising sign (or ascendant) is known as your *descendant*. This shows what you want from other people, and it may give a clue as to your choice of friends, colleagues and lovers (see the chart on page 34). So once you have found your rising sign and read the character interpretation, check out the character reading for your descendant to see what you are looking for in others.

Using the Rising Sign Finder

Please bear in mind that this method is approximate – if you want to be really sure of your rising sign, you should contact an astrologer. However, this system will work with reasonable accuracy wherever you were born, although it is worth checking the Sun and ascendant combination in the following pages and reading the Sun sign character on page 35 for the signs both before and after the rising sign you think is yours. For example, if you think that Capricorn is your rising sign, read the Scorpio/Sagittarius, Scorpio/Capricorn and Scorpio/Aquarius combinations. Then check out the Sun sign character readings for Sagittarius, Capricorn and Aquarius on pages 13, 14 and 15. You will soon see which rising sign fits your personality best.

How to Begin

Read through this section while following the example below. Even if you only have a vague idea of your birth time, you won't find this method difficult; just go for a rough time of birth and then read the Sun sign information for that sign to see if it fits your personality. If you seem to be more like the sign that comes before or after it, then it is likely that you were born a little earlier or later than your assumed time of birth. Don't forget to deduct an hour for summertime births.

1. Look at the illustration below. You will notice that it has the time of day arranged around the outer circle. It looks a bit like a clock face, but it is different because it shows the whole 24–hour day in two-hour blocks.

2. Write the astrological symbol that represents the Sun (a circle with a dot in the middle) in the segment that corresponds to your time of birth. (If you were born during Daylight Saving or British Summer Time, deduct one hour from your birth time.) Our example shows someone who was born between 2 a.m. and 4 a.m.

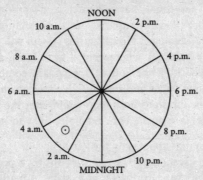

3. Now write the name of your sign or the symbol for your sign on the line which is at the end of the block of time that your Sun falls into. Our example shows a person who was born between 2 a.m. and 4 a.m. under the sign of Pisces.

4. Either write in the names of the zodiac signs or use the symbols in their correct order (see the key on page 34) around the chart in an anti-clockwise direction.

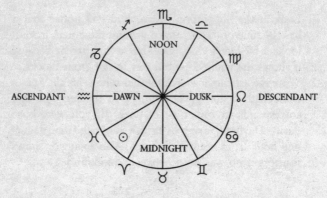

KEY:

♈ Aries	♋ Cancer	♎ Libra	♑ Capricorn
♉ Taurus	♌ Leo	♏ Scorpio	♒ Aquarius
♊ Gemini	♍ Virgo	♐ Sagittarius	♓ Pisces

5. The sign that appears on the left-hand side is your rising sign, or ascendant. The example shows a person born with the Sun in Pisces and with Aquarius rising. Incidentally, the example chart also shows Leo in the descendant.

Here is another example for you to run through, just to make sure that you have grasped the idea correctly. This example is for a more awkward time of birth, being exactly on the line between two different blocks of time. This example is for a person with a Capricorn Sun sign who was born at 10 a.m.

1. The Sun is placed exactly on the 10 a.m. line.
2. The sign of Capricorn is placed on the 10 a.m. line.

3. All the other signs are placed in astrological order (anti-clockwise) around the chart.

4. This person has the Sun in Capricorn and Pisces rising, and therefore with Virgo on the descendant.

How Your Rising Sign Modifies Your Sun Sign
Scorpio with Aries Rising

This powerful combination belongs to a soldier or a person who fights for truth and justice. However, this means that you may miss out a little on family life.

Scorpio with Taurus Rising

You need to love and be loved, but you may have to wait until the right person comes along. You are stubborn but probably not hard to live with.

Scorpio with Gemini Rising

You are attracted to work in an unusual field, such as forensics or some other kind of investigative job. Your nerves are delicate.

Scorpio with Cancer Rising

Home and family are important to you but you are also restless and love to travel over water. You have a great deal of charm and a likeable personality.

Scorpio with Leo Rising

This powerful combination makes you a true leader. You may choose a military life or something similar. You also have impossibly high standards.

Scorpio with Virgo Rising

You are deeply intellectual and you may be keen on medical work or the creation of music or literature. You must watch your sharp tongue.

Scorpio with Libra Rising

This combination attracts you to legal work or, at least to the idea of fair play for all. You could be interested in politics or in helping humanity.

Scorpio with Scorpio Rising

This is Scorpio in its purest form. Your feelings are intensely passionate and you take life seriously. People either love you or hate you. You are even more intuitive if born after dawn, and rather more tough and outgoing if born before.

Scorpio with Sagittarius Rising

You are drawn to mystical or psychic matters and you could be quite eccentric at times. You will travel and meet many interesting people.

Scorpio with Capricorn Rising

You need personal and financial security and you will work hard to get it. You are career-minded, but you also have a good social life.

Scorpio with Aquarius Rising

Work is important to you, and you could be drawn to medical or investigative work. You have plenty of friends and an interesting life. You may be stubborn at times.

Scorpio with Pisces Rising

Your feelings are very strong and also very sensitive. You fear loss or abandonment although you can enjoy your own company when you choose to.

Scorpio in Love

You need:

LOYALTY You fear abandonment and you hate disloyalty in any form. If someone betrays your trust, you never believe in them again.

RESPECT You need a partner whom you can respect and who respects you. You cannot take ridicule and you don't enjoy being in a relationship with a partner who tries to undermine you or who talks down to you in front of others.

PARTNERSHIP You can be the strong one in a relationship but you don't appreciate a lazy partner who leaves everything to you. You need to feel that they are meeting you half way, and that they see the importance of what you are trying to achieve.

You give:

TRUTH You don't lie and you don't bend the truth. If you are not sure of your facts you may say nothing at all, and you do have a tendency to keep your worries to yourself but, when asked, you will tell it as it is.

STEADFASTNESS You stick to a partner through thick and thin and you are a hundred per cent behind his or her endeavours. You work hard and you take relationships seriously.

PASSION You feel deeply about many things and you want a partner who is as committed as you are. Your sexual feelings are strong and you never leave a partner in doubt about your desire for them.

What You Can Expect From the Other Zodiac Signs

ARIES *Truth, honesty, playfulness* You can expect an open and honest relationship with no hidden agendas. Your Arien lover will be a bit childish at times, however.

TAURUS *Security, stability, comfort* The Taurean will stand by you and try to improve your financial position. They will create a beautiful home and garden for you.

GEMINI *Stimulation, encouragement, variety* This lover will never bore you; they give encouragement and are always ready for an outing. They give emotional support too.

CANCER *Emotional security, companionship, help* Cancerians will never leave you stranded at a party or alone when suffering from the flu. They always lend a hand when asked.

LEO *Affection, fun, loyalty* Leo lovers are very steadfast and they would avenge anyone who hurt one of their family. They enjoy romping and playing affectionate love games.

VIRGO *Clear thinking, kindness, humour.* Virgoans make intelligent and amusing partners. They can be critical but are never unkind. They take their responsibility towards you seriously.

LIBRA *Fair-play, sensuality, advice.* Librans will listen to your problems and give balanced and sensible advice. They are wonderfully inventive, and are affectionate lovers too.

SAGITTARIUS *Honesty, fun, novelty.* Theses lovers will never bore you and they'll keep up with whatever pace you set. They seek the truth and they don't keep their feelings hidden.

CAPRICORN *Companionship, common sense, laughter.* Capricorns enjoy doing things together and they won't leave you in the lurch when the going gets tough. They can make you laugh too.

AQUARIUS *Stimulation, friendship, sexuality.* Aquarians are friends as well as lovers. They are great fun because you never know what they are going to do next, in or out of bed.

PISCES *Sympathy, support, love.* These romantic lovers never let you down. They can take you with them into their personal fantasy world and they are always ready for a laugh.

Which Sign Are You Compatible With?

Scorpio/Aries
Hot sexual union but many arguments as each tries to dominate.

Scorpio/Taurus
Shared interests and outlook make this a good combination.

Scorpio/Gemini
Scorpio would dominate and manipulate the Gemini.

Scorpio/Cancer
Much in common and a similar emotional outlook.

Scorpio/Leo
This works well, both are playful and both love a bit of drama.

Scorpio/Virgo
This seems to be a disaster area with both being too critical.

Scorpio/Libra
Not much in common for a love match but all right for work.

Scorpio/Scorpio
Either tremendous harmony or a fight to the death!

Scorpio/Sagittarius
Sagittarius may be too unsettled for Scorpio.

Scorpio/Capricorn
Capricorn can stand up to Scorpio so it works well.

Scorpio/Aquarius
Both extremely obstinate and tense, could be a battleground.

Scorpio/Pisces
Both emotional and intuitive, can have shared interests as well.

Scorpio in 1997

Your Year Ahead

Love

If you are hoping to find love this year, you shouldn't have to travel far from your home to find it. Your locality offers great opportunities for meeting new people both early and late in 1997, while friends could be instrumental in making introductions for you during the remainder of the year. There will be a few hiccups in relationship matters during April and May when communications between you and a lover are likely to become fouled up. Feelings will be running quite high for you and your lover during the spring, so try to avoid confrontations at that time if you can. A secret liaison could become very tricky and awkward during the early summer, and as the year wears on you will decide to become friends rather than to hope for anything more. If someone new comes onto the scene a little later in the year, find the courage to ask them out during the summer and early autumn because you should be agreeably surprised by their response.

Money

It is quite possible that you will start the year with absolutely no intention of moving your home or your business premises, only to find that circumstances change some time during the year. Such a move would prove to be lucky and profitable for you. Some of you may work from home now and this should bring financial success. There is little hope of winning lotteries or gaining through gambles of any kind in 1997, but there will be plenty of work available for you so it should be easy to earn money. Any delays in connection with work or business matters will occur during the summer.

Luck

Your luck this year stems from family matters. If you are setting up a home or getting together with a new love, this will be a pleasant, comfortable and happy affair. Artistic or creative pursuits will go well and any highly original ideas can be cashed in on successfully, especially if these can be carried out in or close to your home. Travel is well starred during the early summer and there shouldn't be any problems associated with travel at any time of the year. You should be able to trust those whom you deal with this year but you will need to take care over legal or other important matters during April and May.

Signs and Symbols

The table at the beginning of each month shows your general trends for the month ahead. The symbols are very easy to understand because the hearts show the state of your love life, the stars tell you how your work is likely to go, the dollar signs tell you whether this will be a good month for money, the heartbeat graphs show your general health and energy levels and the horse shoes tell you whether this will be a lucky month or not.

The Aspects and their Astrological Meanings

CONJUNCT This shows important events which are usually, but not always, good.

SEXTILE Good, particularly for work and mental activity.

SQUARE Difficult, challenging.

TRINE Great for romance, family life and creativity.

OPPOSITE Awkward, depressing, challenging.

INTO This shows when a particular planet enters a new sign of the zodiac, thus setting off a new phase or a new set of circumstances.

DIRECT When a planet resumes normal direct motion.

RETROGRADE When a planet begins to apparently go backwards.

VOID When the Moon makes no aspect to any planet.

January at a Glance

LOVE	♥	♥	♥	♥	
WORK	★	★	★	★	
MONEY	$	$	$	$	
FITNESS	⏧	⏧	⏧		
LUCK	♘				

Wednesday, 1st January
Moon sextile Pluto

It's a good start to the New Year, because something that you loaned to a friend or neighbour should come back today, and something that you mislaid may turn up again. You may do some kind of strange and subtle business deal in which you give someone something, he gives someone else something else and then she gives something back to you. If you see what we mean?

Thursday, 2nd January
Sun conjunct Mercury

There's no doubt that your mental powers are on top form today. The conjunction of the Sun and Mercury lets your intelligence shine. You are particularly persuasive now too, so it shouldn't be difficult to win even the most stubborn and entrenched person over to your cause.

Friday, 3rd January
Mars into Libra

You seem to be entering a placid and peaceful backwater just now, because Mars is disappearing into the quietest area of your chart. However, this is not quite true because you will spend this reflective time working out what you want from life and also making preparations for your future. This is a good time to repay any loans or to fulfil any outstanding obligations.

Saturday, 4th January
Moon sextile Sun

This is a harmonious time when you can express the inner you and find warmth and understanding from those around you. You are charming and persuasive and will certainly be at your best.

Sunday, 5th January
Moon sextile Jupiter

Today should be quite pleasant and there may even be a bit of extra money in the offing for you. You may hear from a far-away friend or relative, or you could find yourself embarking on a pleasant journey.

Monday, 6th January
Mars opposite Saturn

Other people's tendency to drag their feet could be getting you down today. On the other hand, you could be too impatient for your own good. Try to take it easy because one thing is certain . . . you can't force the pace!

Tuesday, 7th January
Moon conjunct Venus

If you're feeling at all weak-willed, don't venture anywhere near expensive shops because you're too prone to the impulse-buying syndrome today. Attractiveness is more important to you than value at the moment, so the temptation to blow your cash on a luxury item is too strong for comfort. Hoard your resources now and leave shopping trips until you're less impetuous.

Wednesday, 8th January
Moon conjunct Mercury

You might think that you speak in a reasoned, clear voice today, but your emotional intensity is showing through. You've obviously got a lot of conviction now and you can't fail to be persuasive and eloquent when you display such sincerity. If a close partnership has been going through a sticky patch, then it's time you expressed your true feelings.

Thursday, 9th January
Jupiter conjunct Neptune

Your thoughts will be tinged with spirituality today as Jupiter gets together with Neptune in your house of ideas. An interest in religion could be stimulated, although in matters of belief a more non-conformist viewpoint is likely to be adopted. You may also feel a strong desire to travel to somewhere that has personal and spiritual significance.

Friday, 10th January
Venus into Capricorn

If you've got any favours to ask, the passage of Venus into your solar house of persuasion shows that you can use considerable charm and eloquence to easily win others over to your point of view. A little flirtation combined with a winning way ensures that you achieve your desires. Your creative talents are boosted too, so perhaps you should consider writing down your inspirations.

Saturday, 11th January
Venus square Saturn

You may be feeling a bit under the weather today, or you

may simply not be the in the mood for the work that you have to get through. The best approach is to keep to your usual routine and not try anything that requires much effort for the time being. A woman and a person in a position of authority will be closeted together for hours at work, leaving you excluded from their charmed circle.

Sunday, 12th January
Mercury direct

A lot of tension is dissipated as Mercury resumes direct motion today. This is a good chance to sort out misunderstandings, unravel confused thinking and get more mobile. Short trips that lead to happy meetings are the favoured activity today.

Monday, 13th January
Moon sextile Sun

It's a day for simple pleasures and innocent enjoyment. A quiet conversation with a child or younger person should show you that you can still learn a thing or two, and have a laugh as well.

Tuesday, 14th January
Moon square Venus

Tuesday looks like a lethargic day for usually active Scorpios. It's obvious that you've bitten off far more than you can chew in a work situation and are now suffering the after effects. You won't want to be bothered with anything strenuous today.

Wednesday, 15th January
Mercury square Mars

Those around you may be saying one thing but actually doing something completely different. You are also aware that your logical mind and your inner voice are going in two different directions. You may find that this is a very confusing and irritating situation to deal with.

Thursday, 16th January
Moon square Uranus

You could suffer a bit of tension in or around the home today. Older family members may be making one set of demands upon you, while a partner may be making another. You cannot tear yourself in two, so somebody is going to be disappointed. If you really want to set the cat among the pigeons, go out with a friend and leave them all to squabble!

Friday, 17th January
Sun conjunct Neptune

You're extremely perceptive under the mixed rays of the Sun/Neptune conjunction today. You'll instinctively know what lies behind the most confusing smokescreen. People will hardly open their mouths before you know exactly what they want, why and if it's a good idea or not. You've obviously got a powerful sixth sense and your insights border on the psychic levels of awareness. Be sure you put this ability to good use.

Saturday, 18th January
Moon sextile Saturn

You will make a couple of minor changes in your approach to the way you do your chores today. You may decide to tidy the place up a bit and to recycle what can be reused and throw out all the useless junk that is cluttering the place up.

Sunday, 19th January
Sun conjunct Jupiter

There is good news about a number of things on the way

to you now. There may be something positive happening in connection with a legal matter today, or possibly money coming in from something to do with contracts or documents. You may receive a tax rebate or an insurance payment. New opportunities will arise and useful new contacts can be made now.

Monday, 20th January
Sun into Aquarius

The home and family become your main interest over the next four weeks as the Sun moves into the most domestic area of your chart from today. Family feuds will now be resolved, and you'll find an increasing contentment in your own surroundings. A haven of peace will be restored in your home. This should also be a period of nostalgia when happy memories come flooding back.

Tuesday, 21st January
Jupiter into Aquarius

Your innate kindness and compassion for others is being stimulated now by the entry of Jupiter in your solar area of family, home and heritage. Your protective instincts will be strongly stimulated in the coming months. However, you may tend to be rather possessive, not allowing loved ones an opportunity to stand on their own two feet.

Wednesday, 22nd January
Mars sextile Pluto

Financial matters will benefit from some forethought today. You'd be wise to turn your shrewd mind to the prospect of encouraging your bank balance. The chances are that you can make savings on unnecessary expenses and relieve yourself of unwanted debts.

Thursday, 23rd January
Full Moon

Today's Full Moon shows that important decisions have to be made at a time of rapidly changing circumstances. News that arrives today could be disturbing, yet will prove to be a blessing in disguise in the long run. You may be considering a move of home, possibly to a distant location, or even throwing in your present career to take up an educational course of some kind. People you meet while travelling will have important words to say.

Friday, 24th January
Sun conjunct Uranus

If you were expecting a peaceful day around the house, then think again! Anything could happen today. Unexpected visitors, a sudden urge to redecorate the kitchen or a disastrous dish that turns into something else. Just go with the flow and take it all as it comes!

Saturday, 25th January
Sun trine Mars

Sometimes you have to plan for someone else, especially when they don't seem at all inclined to do it for themselves. You might seem like a tyrant laying down the law, but you are actually right and it's high time that a family member realised it!

Sunday, 26th January
Mars trine Uranus

Something out of the blue could take you by surprise today; for example, you may have unexpected visitors or a pleasantly surprising invitation to somewhere unusual. Friends may drop in or they may contact you with exciting news. Single women may be taken by storm by a

distinguished man who sweeps into your life in the most
odd and unexpected manner.

Monday, 27th January
Moon trine Venus

A chat with a woman friend may be just the thing to help
you get things into perspective today. You seem to need
some kind of practical advice in order to prevent you from
taking a rather foolish course of action. A pal may suggest
an outing later in the day, and you'll be missing a lot of
fun if you turn this down.

Tuesday, 28th January
Moon trine Jupiter

Your home and domestic circumstances are really rather
good at present, and whatever you have in mind for
yourself and your family will go particularly well today.
You may be keen to move house now or to put an existing
home into some kind of order, and it looks as though the
opportunity to do this is fast approaching.

Wednesday, 29th January
Moon square Mercury

Your mind is racing so fast you can't help causing
misunderstandings just now. You may also receive some
wounding criticism, although you must admit that you're
being a touch over-sensitive. If these hurtful words were
actually meant to be constructive, then you could do worse
than think hard about the issues they raise.

Thursday, 30th January
Moon square Neptune

If you are the sort of person who puts little credence in
the world of psychic awareness, you could be in for
something of a shock today as a revelation is in store.

You're intrigued by mysteries now, and no mystery is more alluring than that of your subconscious mind. Dreams and visions are the order of the day, and whether you believe that your messages come from the other world or your inner self, their truth will stand out in the face of even the harshest logic.

Friday, 31st January
Moon square Uranus

Guard against accidents in the home today. If you have to clamber upwards in order to get at something, then make sure you use a proper step-ladder rather than perching perilously on a rickety stool. A mother-figure may say something to annoy you, and because your confidence is at a rather low ebb, you may be tempted to snap back at her defensively. This may be a good thing, who knows?

February at a Glance

LOVE	♥				
WORK	★	★	★	★	
MONEY	$	$	$		
FITNESS	◉				
LUCK	U	U	U	U	U

Saturday, 1st February
Venus conjunct Neptune

There are bound to be lots of misunderstandings today. Venus unites with Neptune now, making the most innocent comment a minefield of misinformation and crossed purposes. It'll be difficult for you to explain yourself clearly, especially when you start getting flashes of psychic awareness. At the best of times this can be difficult to put into words, but today your instincts are almost impossible to express.

Sunday, 2nd February
Moon conjunct Pluto

You seem to be getting a grip on your money situation now. You may have been allowing things to slip, spending too much on those credit and debit cards or simply not taking enough notice of what is going in and out of your bank account. This is the time to put the brakes on any overspending and to get your finances back into shape once again.

Monday, 3rd February
Venus into Aquarius

Old scores and family squabbles can now be laid to rest as the passage of Venus into your domestic area signals a time of harmony and contentment. Surround yourself with beauty, both in terms of affection and material possessions. This is a good time to renew a closeness with those you love. Join forces to complete a major project such as redecoration, or even a move of home. Be assured that the stars smile on you now.

Tuesday, 4th February
Moon square Saturn

You may feel under the weather or simply over-tired today. The chances are that you have not been sleeping too well recently, and this seems to be taking its toll today in terms of fatigue. You may have been burning the candle at both ends, and now there isn't enough candle left to light your way home.

Wednesday, 5th February
Uranus sextile Pluto

If you have been wanting to make improvements to your home but haven't had the money to do so, things could be changing for the better now. You will soon have an opportunity to go out and buy what you want, or to acquire what you need very cheaply from some unexpected and unusual source.

Thursday, 6th February
Mars retrograde

That highly charged and over-energetic planet Mars seems to have gone to sleep as far as your horoscope is concerned. The next few weeks are not wonderful times to start new projects because you won't have either the energy or the enterprise for it. Take time to step back from the rough-and-tumble of life. Retreat and reflect before tackling any demanding tasks.

Friday, 7th February
New Moon

The New Moon falls in the sphere of home and family today indicating a need for a change. For some reason you've been dissatisfied with your domestic set-up so you may consider looking at house prices in your own, or indeed another area. You probably feel that you need more space and light in your life that your present home isn't providing. A family member may be considering setting up home for themselves, and they deserve all the encouragement you can give.

Saturday, 8th February
Mercury conjunct Neptune

It's a fairly confusing day, we're afraid. Mercury is in close conjunction with Neptune which garbles your message and leaves you tongue-tied. It's so irritating, because you have such wonderful ideas to share. It's a pity that no one else understands what you're on about today.

Sunday, 9th February
Jupiter sextile Saturn

The dream home is possible, that's the astral message now! You will realise that everything you want for your house is within reach, even if you know that you have to work hard to get it. Dealings with older members of your family should be smooth and productive too.

Monday, 10th February
Moon conjunct Saturn

There will be good news for you at work today. You may be given a rise, a promotion or a word or two of praise from a superior. You will look back on work that you have completed and be pleased with the results. This is a good time to finish one round of work and to start on another, so get going on new projects now both in your work and at home.

Tuesday, 11th February
Mercury conjunct Jupiter

Today is a good day for travelling or to make travel arrangements, and this goes for local and long-distance journeys. Nevertheless, it is worth taking the precaution of paying a bit more in order to get tickets that can be changed or refunded if necessary. This is also a pretty good day to deal with business or money matters, or to sign important papers.

Wednesday, 12th February
Moon square Neptune

It won't take much to discourage you today. Your mood is on the sombre side and you'll be looking for excuses simply because your image has taken a knock. Of course there's not much substance in your fears, so walk tall and put your anxieties in perspective.

Thursday, 13th February
Mercury conjunct Uranus

You are likely to be surprised by the antics of various family members today, and your mother or grandparents are the most likely source of all the fun. You may hear some really unexpected news about these relatives and they could suddenly decide to descend upon you to give you their glad tidings.

Friday, 14th February
Jupiter sextile Pluto

To make your dreams come true you have to ditch certain outworn obligations. Perhaps you ought to think about trimming back the luxuries for a while until you have achieved your aims? A good domestic spring-clean could be therapeutic.

Saturday, 15th February
Mars opposite Saturn

Although you will want to make colleagues work harder, they'll be extremely resistant to any urging on your part. The best thing to do is to work at your own pace and let them work at theirs. However, this could be pretty frustrating if your work is dependent on their actions!

Sunday, 16th February
Jupiter conjunct Uranus

A surprising turn of events in the family will have a very positive outcome. Possibly some member of your family will have a windfall or some other stroke of luck that will benefit you.

Monday, 17th February
Moon square Mars

You might not realise it, but you are quite argumentative today. You may think that you've concealed your worries, but the tension is getting to you, and you're making sure that those around you are getting their share of it as well. It may be that you aren't aware of the root cause of your mood swings, so spend some time analysing your reactions. You'll soon discover the reason for your anxiety.

Tuesday, 18th February
Sun into Pisces

You are going to be in a slightly frivolous frame of mind over the next few weeks, and you shouldn't punish yourself for this! Pay attention to a creative interest or a demanding hobby now or get involved in something creative on behalf of others. A couple of typical examples would be the production of a school play or making preparations for a flower and vegetable show.

Wednesday, 19th February
Saturn trine Pluto

Sentimentality has no place when you are trying so hard to be practical. The way you have done things in the past may no longer fit present needs, so it's time to accept change, no matter how disruptive it might be.

Thursday, 20th February
Moon opposite Jupiter

If you are looking for a job today, you could be disappointed. Don't take this too seriously; it may be that the people you have applied to could use you, but at a later date, or that it's not the kind of job that you want anyway. The same goes for your chances of promotion or a rise because there are simply better days on which to get a favourable response.

Friday, 21st February
Moon opposite Venus

Your life needs some kind of alteration or rearranging now. You are shouldering too many burdens now, both at home and at work and you will need to deal with this soon before you feel too pressurised. You may need more assistance from those around you, so you may take on extra staff to help out.

Saturday, 22nd February
Full Moon

Today's Full Moon could make you feel a bit tetchy and tense, and it could also bring you some sort of unexpected expense. The best thing to do today is to stick to your usual routine and not start anything new or important. Jog along as usual and try not to let anybody else's bad mood affect you now.

Sunday, 23rd February
Sun square Pluto

Your willpower is at its weakest today as the Sun makes a harsh aspect to Pluto, making your desires outstrip your capacity to fulfil them. We know that there's nothing you'd like better than a holiday, a trip to the theatre or a riotous night out, but if the bank balance won't stand it, you'll have to be more economical. Grumbling won't help when financial realities have to be faced.

Monday, 24th February
Moon conjunct Mars

Early on in the day you'll be keeping a lot of unexpressed frustration under control. However, internal pressure is building. It's no answer to keep negative feelings bottled up, but exploding in all directions isn't a good idea either. Direct your anger at the root cause of the problem rather than taking it out on all around you. You'll be tempted to plot an intricate revenge, but you should try to prove your detractors wrong by doing the best you can.

Tuesday, 25th February
Moon opposite Saturn

You may not be feeling at your best today, so slow down, take some time off and coddle yourself a little. You may have the start of a summer cold or some kind of ailment, such as backache. This isn't likely to be a wonderful day as far as work is concerned, so be sensible and rest if you can.

Wednesday, 26th February
Moon square Neptune

You may put yourself out for others only to find that they are unappreciative. Don't make a martyr of yourself today, but make sure that you acknowledge those who put themselves out on your behalf now.

Thursday, 27th February
Venus into Pisces

This is a good day to begin new projects and to get great ideas off the ground. Venus is now moving into the area of your chart that is concerned with creativity, so over the next few weeks you can take advantage of this and get involved with some kind of creative process. Venus is concerned with beauty, so utilise this planetary energy to enhance your work now.

Friday, 28th February
Mercury into Pisces

The creative trend continues as Mercury moves into a part of your horoscope that is concerned with creativity. Mercury rules such things as thinking, learning and communications, but it can also be associated with skills and craft work of various kinds. This combination suggests that the next few weeks would be a good time to work on hobbies such as dressmaking, carpentry and so on.

March at a Glance

LOVE	♥	♥	♥	♥	♥
WORK	★	★			
MONEY	$				
FITNESS	〜	〜	〜	〜	
LUCK	∪	∪	∪	∪	

Saturday, 1st March
Saturn sextile Uranus

Today's excellent aspect between Saturn and Uranus is the start of a rather good phase. This will bring you long-term success in domestic affairs. Whatever it is that you want to achieve, you will soon have the power and energy to do so.

Sunday, 2nd March
Moon square Sun

Go easy on your expenditure today. Avoid the shops, don't go looking for bargains and don't let anybody else talk you into buying anything either. Older relatives may be a bit irritating today, possibly because they need you to do something for them which means using up a lot of your spare time. It would be better to spend today attending to your duties rather than seeking out amusement.

Monday, 3rd March
Venus square Pluto

Being fond of someone is one thing, but letting your feelings become too intense is quite another. And that's the trend that has to be combated today, for the aspect between Venus and Pluto heightens your affections. Try to keep a measure of common sense and you won't go far wrong, but give in to your impulses and you'll find yourself in no end of trouble.

Tuesday, 4th March
Mercury conjunct Venus

Your love life looks up today when a charming and flirtatious mood takes a hold. You'll be extremely seductive and will win admiration with ease. Your silver tongue enables you to express pent-up feelings.

Wednesday, 5th March
Moon conjunct Neptune

Your heart is filled with compassion for others today. Maybe you want to help someone in particular, or perhaps you feel drawn to raise money for a good cause. You may find it hard to concentrate now, because daydreams are coming between you and your everyday duties.

Thursday, 6th March
Moon conjunct Jupiter

Some members of your family seem to look at you as a sort of super-hero at the moment. While this is rather flattering, it's also inaccurate. You can't actually manage to do everything they want no matter how much this flatters your ego. Keep a firm grip on reality rather than believing in your own publicity!.

Friday, 7th March
Mars into Virgo retrograde

Mars makes a kind of backwards move into the area of your chart that is devoted to acquaintanceships. This may throw you back into the arms of friends and colleagues rather than into the company of lovers and family members. Group activities will demand your attention and you may have to give up some time in order to serve on a committee or to help out at a local event.

Saturday, 8th March
Pluto retrograde

Pluto, the planet of transformations, goes into one of its periodical backwards phases from today, and this influence helps you to get your material affairs in order. Apart from mere money, the dark planet encourages an examination of what makes you feel worthwhile. You've got a few months to sort out your priorities, starting from today.

Sunday, 9th March
New Moon eclipse

Eclipses are quite difficult things to live with. The Romans used to dread them, saying that they brought bad times in their wake. However, there are usually two lunar and two solar eclipses each year so they aren't that unusual. Problems come when these fall on sensitive areas of one's birth chart. If this eclipse catches you out, then it will cut short a celebration or some kind of leisure activity.

Monday, 10th March
Sun conjunct Mercury

Communication is the name of the game today as this will enhance all your relationships. You could have a really enjoyable chat to a friend, or you could sit and talk things over with your lover. You may decide to start a creative venture now and, if so, this is the time to research your ideas to see what materials and methods would best suit your purpose.

Tuesday, 11th March
Moon square Neptune

If you're feeling under the weather today, there won't be much point in blaming bugs or germs. It's more than likely that the symptoms you're experiencing can be put down to stress. There's only one effective cure and that's relaxation, so be kind to yourself and take it easy for once!

Wednesday, 12th March
Moon square Uranus

If you are a solo operator and would like to become a part of a couple then do take things easily today, because if you're too eager you may frighten away a potential lover. Nobody likes to think that they are simply filling a gap – we all want to be loved irresistibly just for who we are, and not simply because someone else needs a partner.

Thursday, 13th March
Moon sextile Sun

This is a good time for your love life. If you are deeply committed then you should share quality time with your partner. If single, then today could bring you into contact with someone who will become very important romantically. But remember to play it cool!

Friday, 14th March
Moon opposite Pluto

Guard against being talked into buying anything today. Avoid slick salesmen (or women) like the plague, and don't agree to anything on the phone or on the doorstep in order to get the vendor off your back. You need to think carefully about any kind of joint agreement or business matter, but you must avoid being rail-roaded into anything that is against your own interests.

Saturday, 15th March
Moon square Venus

You and your lover seem to be sorting out some of your problems now and this is definitely the time to kiss and make up. Fortunately for you, the making up is likely to lead to an outburst of sheer passion, so make the most of each other's company while your libidos are so in tune. You may be asked to invest in a glamorous scheme, and although this looks like a dodgy idea, it may be worth taking a small chance.

Sunday, 16th March
Mercury into Aries

The movement of Mercury into your solar sixth house of work, duties and health suggests that a slightly more serious phase is on the way. Over the next three weeks or so you will have to concentrate on what needs to be done rather than on having a good time. You may have a fair bit to do with neighbours, colleagues and relatives of around your own age group soon, and you'll have to spend time on the 'phone to them.

Monday, 17th March
Sun opposite Mars

If you are trying to do something interesting in the company of others today, then you could feel frustrated and disappointed by their lack of enthusiasm for your pet project. Friends may suddenly decide to leave you to get on with things alone, and you could feel neglected as a result. You may even find yourself in opposition to a group of people.

Tuesday, 18th March
Moon opposite Neptune

Sometimes the world doesn't live up to your high standards. But before you become demoralised, think hard about the message your fate is sending you; perhaps you feel that you've embarked on the wrong course, or dealing with people who don't share your ideals? Understanding the problem is indeed half way to solving it. Look on the bright side!

Wednesday, 19th March
Moon opposite Uranus

A sudden and unexpected event could send you scurrying home from work in order to sort out a domestic crisis. Alternatively, you may not be able to get home at your usual time due to a crisis at your place of work. One of your superiors could be shunted out of his or her job, leaving a mass of work entirely in your hands. If this is the case, you may find that your family are less than sympathetic to your plight.

Thursday, 20th March
Sun into Aries

The Sun moves into your solar sixth house of work and duty for the next month. This solar movement will encourage you to concentrate on your health and well-being and that of your family too. If you are off-colour, the Sun will help you to get back to full health once again. If you have outstanding jobs to do, the next month or so will be a good time for action.

Friday, 21st March
Mercury conjunct Saturn

Your status at work is about to reach new heights today, and anything that you propose will be taken very seriously. You may receive praise and recognition for past efforts and you could see the results of a long-term project. People who are in positions of authority will be pleased with your work and you will feel quite satisfied with your progress.

Saturday, 22nd March
Mercury sextile Jupiter

If you work hard and keep your nose firmly attached to the grindstone today you will achieve your aims with more speed and efficiency than usual. You may receive some kind of formal reward for past and present efforts, but it is equally possible that you will feel satisfied with a job well done.

Sunday, 23rd March
Venus into Aries

Venus moves out of the fun, sun and pleasure area of your chart into the work, duty and health area, and it will stay there for the next few weeks. This suggests that any problems related to work and duty will become easier to handle, and also that you could start to see some kind of practical outcome from all that you have been doing lately. If you have been feeling under the weather recently, Venus will help you to feel better soon.

Monday, 24th March
Full Moon eclipse

Today's eclipse concentrates on your working life, showing you that it may be time to call a halt to any activity that isn't giving you sufficient reward or satisfaction. If your health's been troubling you then it's time to get the problem sorted out once and for all. Ignoring an ache won't make it go away; it's better to visit your doctor if only to set your mind at rest. A complete change of routine could also be a help.

Tuesday, 25th March
Moon opposite Mercury

If you are engaged in a long and detailed task such as dressmaking, do-it-yourself or craft work of some kind, you may find the going difficult today. You could encounter unexpected hitches or you may decide to set the whole job aside for a while to do something more important. Work of all kinds could be frustrating for at least some part of the day.

Wednesday, 26th March
Moon square Neptune

You are so sensitive today that you should keep well away from moody and miserable people. You could also be somewhat gullible, so do try to resist sob stories.

Thursday, 27th March
Moon square Jupiter

This is not the time to gamble on anything. Stick to tried and tested methods and don't overreach yourself in any way. If you go out on a limb now, you could risk everything that you have worked so hard to achieve. You may need to spend some extra money on your home or on a mother figure today.

Friday, 28th March
Moon conjunct Pluto

A change in your luck will bring you an excellent opportunity this Good Friday. This could be money for you or your loved ones, but it could just as easily be the path to a good job or some other improvement to your position. Someone may manipulate or manoeuvre a situation to help you – and all this for no perceptible reward!

Saturday, 29th March
Moon trine Venus

From now on, it's possible that an office romance or a chance meeting at work could turn into love! Even if this is not the case, you could enjoy a gentle flirtation with the delivery girl or the man who calls round to your workplace. There should be good will and kindness around you at work and among anyone whom you work with in a voluntary capacity.

Sunday, 30th March
Sun sextile Uranus

A Great Easter Sunday! You can now begin to make sense of both your home and your work situation and friends may come up with solutions for problems in both of these areas of your life. You may be given an opportunity to buy something for the home at a real knock-down price and parents could even come up with a way to transport it.

Monday, 31st March
Sun conjunct Saturn

This is the day to launch long-term action plans and to work towards making your job more fruitful. You may look into the acquisition of machinery to make your job easier, or a new marketing strategy which will increase or improve the status of your product or services. This is a good day to take on staff or even to find a new job for yourself if you need to.

April at a Glance

LOVE	♥	♥	♥		
WORK	★				
MONEY	$	$	$	$	$
FITNESS	〰				
LUCK	☊	☊	☊	☊	☊

Tuesday, 1st April
Mercury into Taurus

The inquisitive Mercury moves into your solar house of marriage and long-lasting relationships from today, ushering in a period when a renewed understanding can be reached between you and your partner. New relationships can be formed under this influence too, although these will tend to be on a light, fairly superficial level. Good humour and plenty of chat should be a feature for a few weeks, but you must try to curb a tendency to needlessly criticise another's foibles. Remember, not even you are perfect!

Wednesday, 2nd April
Sun conjunct Venus

The astral vibes are pretty good when the Sun gets together with Venus. You feel on top of the world and ready for anything. The only problem is that you have such an appetite for the good life that you could easily overdo it. Have fun by all means, but don't indulge yourself so much that you'll regret it in the morning.

Thursday, 3rd April
Sun sextile Jupiter

There is a feeling of luck and opportunity around you now. If illness has plagued you recently, then you should now start to feel much better. The same goes for other members of your family. There will be new contacts to be made and new opportunities finding their way to your doorstep, both at work and at home.

Friday, 4th April
Moon sextile Mercury

It's time for fun and togetherness as the Moon and Mercury highlight romantic potentials and partnerships. Forget mundane worries and get out with the sole aim of enjoying yourself. The presence of someone special makes this a time to remember.

Saturday, 5th April
Moon opposite Mars

Boredom is the enemy today because you're likely to react in an impulsive and even destructive way to anything that holds you down. The fault lies with the lunar opposition to Mars which gives you irrepressible energy, but limits your outlets. If your hobbies or leisure activities aren't giving you the satisfaction you crave, you should consider a new way to express yourself and regain some enthusiasm for life.

Sunday, 6th April
Moon trine Pluto

If you have recently lost or mislaid anything, it should turn up again today. The same mysterious force that took your possessions away from you will operate in the other direction today, by just as mysteriously returning them! You should receive good news about work and also about any health matters that have been bothering you recently.

Monday, 7th April
New Moon

Today's New Moon gives you the stamina to shrug off any minor ailments that have been troubling you. Occurring, as it does, in your solar house of health and work, it's obvious that you need to get yourself into shape to face the challenges that await you. A few early nights, a better diet and a readiness to give up bad habits such as smoking will work wonders.

Tuesday, 8th April
Mercury square Uranus

An irritable atmosphere prevails around the home today, and though you may not be aware of it you are as much to blame as your partner. To avoid any further unpleasantness, try to restrain your tongue. A tactless remark could have unforeseen consequences!

Wednesday, 9th April
Moon trine Mars

You can't seem to do any wrong at the moment. There are

lots of people around who will bend over backwards to help you along. There's plenty of encouragement and appreciation from friends and colleagues who wish you well. If you're self-confidence is on a low, you can be sure that you're the only one who takes a negative view of your situation.

Thursday, 10th April
Moon trine Neptune

Someone whom you chat to on a regular basis may take you by surprise by suddenly declaring feelings of love for you. This may delight you or it could unsettle you, depending upon who it is and how their feelings are expressed.

Friday, 11th April
Moon trine Jupiter

This should be a pleasant day with some rather nice surprises both at home and in the outside world. Your partner may cheer you up by suggesting that you book a holiday, or that you plan a pleasant trip of some kind. There may be a bit more money on the way to the family coffers, or you may find that your debts are not as great as you had expected.

Saturday, 12th April
Moon sextile Venus

What a romantic and loving day this is. However, you are in such a soppy mood that you may find yourself agreeing to do something for your lover that under other, more sober circumstances, you would never agree to at all.

Sunday, 13th April
Moon sextile Mercury

Your mind is ticking over with new concepts and ideas

that you hadn't thought of before. Philosophical to a fault, you'll be mulling over the deeper meanings of subjects raised recently. Whether your interest is political, religious or more obscure, I'm sure you'll find your partner is interested in anything you have to say. This is an excellent day to think about travel plans.

Monday, 14th April
Moon square Sun

You have the promise of high achievement coming up, but it's important that you don't overload your schedule or take on far more than you can comfortably cope with. It's very tempting to push hard now, but watch out for the law of diminishing returns. The more you take on, the more tired you'll be and the harder the effort needed to complete your tasks. Be easy on yourself. Everything is going well, so coast along with it. You don't need to store up stressful problems for the future.

Tuesday, 15th April
Mercury retrograde

In all partnerships, both business and those of a more personal nature, misunderstandings, crossed purposes and ill-timed words are likely as Mercury embarks on a retrograde course from today. The next few weeks could see a lot of confusion, so you must be crystal-clear in all you say, otherwise arguments will result simply because someone has got the wrong end of the stick.

Wednesday, 16th April
Venus into Taurus

Venus, the planet of romance, moves into your horoscopic area of close relationships from today, increasing your physical desires and bringing the light of love into your heart. If you're involved in a long-term partnership it's a chance to renew the magic of the early days of your union. If single, then the next few weeks should bring a stunning new attraction into your life.

Thursday, 17th April
Moon trine Sun

In all career affairs today should be plain sailing. Harmony reigns with your bosses and co-workers so no matter how arduous the task, you'll find that everyone is in agreement. For once, you're perfectly content to carry on with routine duties. It may not be an exciting outlook but it is familiar and you'll be quite comfortable with that.

Friday, 18th April
Moon trine Mercury

There is no need to compartmentalise your world now, so allow your friends to meet your lover and vice versa. You may fear losing your beloved to one of your more charming pals, but this is highly unlikely. Your friends will respect the fact that you feel deeply about your lover and they will want to keep your friendship too.

Saturday, 19th April
Sun square Neptune

The Sun's square aspect to Neptune warns against taking on too much, and overloading your already overburdened schedule. The trouble is that you feel you can handle anything the world throws at you, but you aren't taking the physical toll into account. Slow down for once, and let others shoulder some of the burden for you. Your health should be your first priority, not whether you get the job done more quickly.

Sunday, 20th April
Sun into Taurus

The Sun moves into the area of your chart devoted to relationships from today. If things have been difficult in a partnership, either personal or business, then this is your chance to put everything back in its proper place. It's obvious that the significant other in your life deserves respect and affection and that's just what you're now prepared to give. Teamwork is the key to success over the next month.

Monday, 21st April
Mercury square Uranus

Tension in the home could be caused by a frank statement that tresspasses into tactlessness. Forthright speech is acceptable in some situations, but this isn't one of them. Timing is all!

Tuesday, 22nd April
Full Moon

Today's Full Moon suggests that all is not well with at least one personal relationship. You may find someone close to you acting in a particularly awkward manner now, or you may find that it is impossible for you to get through to them.

Wednesday, 23rd April
Venus square Uranus

You are supposed to be incredibly patient now, but it doesn't mean that you are immune to stress. Today you will be busy playing the role of a discrete peacemaker. You won't be able to keep this up for long, so there could be an outburst of volcanic proportions!

Thursday, 24th April
Moon square Jupiter

Don't take anything on face value today. The outlook may be optimistic but there are hidden pitfalls so tread warily. In all domestic and family matters, keep out of matters that don't concern you.

Friday, 25th April
Sun conjunct Mercury

You and your lover have a great deal to talk over and today is the day to do it. If you are in the early stages of a relationship, you will find that you have a great deal in common and you will be able to while away many happy hours together discussing your childhoods and backgrounds. If you have something that is niggling you, don't keep it to yourself because it will linger there, possibly causing long-term resentment.

Saturday, 26th April
Moon sextile Jupiter

Money-wise and in dealings with authority you're in luck today. A marvellous astral combination ensures that you won't take the less-than-perfect, and you are forceful and assertive. Just make sure that you don't take this wilfulness too far or you could end up dishing out far more than anyone deserves. At the very least you are going to get what you want.

Sunday, 27th April
Mars direct

Mars turns to direct motion in your solar house of friendship and acquaintanceship. If you have lost any friends over the last few weeks, then this is the time to get out and make new ones. You may join a club or society soon, or you may team up with a group of people who share your hopes, wishes and beliefs. Lonely ladies who are reading this stand more chance of meeting a new love now that Mars is on your side once again.

Monday, 28th April
Sun square Uranus

You need the co-operation of those around you today, but acting like a petty tyrant isn't going to win you any brownie points, especially with your other half. Think before you act if you want to avoid trouble.

Tuesday, 29th April
Moon square Mercury

No sooner does Mercury open channels of communication than you're back into a cycle of misunderstanding and mistrust. Perhaps you aren't trying hard enough to express your feelings? Take it slowly; wounds don't heal in ten minutes, so use the gentle touch to renew trust.

Wednesday, 30th April
Venus trine Mars

A great day for pouring oil on troubled waters where relationships are concerned. The Venusian aspect to Mars shows that you should treat that special person to a night out on the town to renew a little of the old romance. If you are unattached, then this is the perfect time to find a prospective partner.

May at a Glance

LOVE	♥	♥	♥	♥	
WORK	★	★	★		
MONEY	$	$	$		
FITNESS	🫀	🫀			
LUCK	☵	☵			

Thursday, 1st May
Neptune retrograde
You may find it quite hard to concentrate or to focus your mind on anything in particular over the next few months. You know that you have decisions to take and choices to make, but you may feel vaguely paralysed by the very thought of it.

Friday, 2nd May
Venus square Jupiter
You will find it hard to keep the peace at home today. Your partner and your parents (or his parents) are at loggerheads, and nothing you can do will put things right. You can only wait for them to get over their bad moods.

Saturday, 3rd May
Mercury square Neptune
Your own better nature could lead you astray today because it would be too easy to convince you of anything. Although you are willing to help anyone out, a person who asks for your aid now may not deserve it.

Sunday, 4th May
Moon conjunct Saturn

Something important is happening at work. You may be given a more responsible job with an increase in salary and status to go with it. You could be in a position to hire some help now and, if so, you will find just the right person for the job. Any changes that take place now in connection with work, chores or even housework will be for the better.

Monday, 5th May
Mercury into Aries retrograde

Mercury's return to your solar house of health and habits may encourage you to take a good look at your physical well-being. This is a good time to get yourself checked over from top to toe, just to make sure that everything's in fine working order.

Tuesday, 6th May
New Moon

The only planetary activity today is a New Moon in your opposite sign. It is possible that this could bring the start of a new relationship for the lonely but, to be honest, this planetary aspect is a bit too weak for such a big event. It is much more likely that you will improve upon a current relationship rather than embark on a new romance at this particular time.

Wednesday, 7th May
Sun trine Mars

It will be very easy to deal with other people today because they will be in a mood to co-operate with your schemes and dreams. You can expect help and advice from someone who is in a powerful position now, and your own status will increase in some kind of strange and rather subtle manner too.

Thursday, 8th May
Mercury direct

You should feel less on edge and generally more healthy as Mercury gets back on course from today. Apart from this, a friend may be pressurising you to get you to do something that you're not at all keen on. Fortunately Mercury's forward motion should ensure that you have the eloquence to defuse the situation without ruffling any feathers.

Friday, 9th May
Moon trine Jupiter

A calmer and more peaceful atmosphere is prevailing around you at the moment. You seem to be able to get onto the right wavelength with your partner and your family now, and everyone is co-operating with everyone else for once.

Saturday, 10th May
Venus into Gemini

Venus enters the area of your chart that is concerned with love and sex. Oddly enough, this aspect can bring the end of a difficult relationship, or just as easily begin a wonderful new romance. If you have been dating but haven't yet got around to 'mating', this could be the start of something wonderful. Your emotional life over the next two or three weeks should be something to remember, that's for sure!

Sunday, 11th May
Sun square Jupiter

Oh boy, today is going to be an expensive one! Something

is going to be more costly than you had bargained for and that 'affordable' luxury is likely to be a real drain on your resources. If this isn't enough, your partner may take a dim view of your sudden desire to live like a millionaire. Try to avoid ending the day falling out over this.

Monday, 12th May
Mercury into Taurus

Mercury moves into the area of your chart which is concerned with relationships that are open and above-board now. This suggests that over the next few weeks you will have nothing to be secretive about in connection with your relationships with others. Your friendships will be free and easy and your lovers the kind whom you can happily take home to mother!

Tuesday, 13th May
Uranus retrograde

Your own surroundings hold little appeal as the erratic Uranus begins a retrograde course today. You're afflicted by wanderlust, but for one reason or another, you can't quite get organised enough to do anything about it. If you aren't careful this restless attitude could come over as rebellion, as you reject what you know in favour of the new and exciting. Patience may be a dirty word to you, yet you'd be wise to use some, especially since this mood will soon pass and you could be left with a rather resentful family around you.

Wednesday, 14th May
Venus opposite Pluto

You may find it hard to express your feelings to the one you love today. It is possible that you could try to sort out a number of financial or practical difficulties between you and your lover now, only to find that he or she walks away from you and does not want to listen to what you feel you have to say.

Thursday, 15th May
Moon square Venus

If you fancy an undemanding day with plenty of peace and harmony, I'm afraid you're due for a rude awakening. No one has the slightest intention of leaving you to your own devices now. Well-meaning friends will urge you to be social, but all they manage to do is make you irritable. If you really do crave solitude you'll have to unplug the phone, ignore the door bell and pretend to be out.

Friday, 16th May
Moon conjunct Mars

Women in particular have a terrific opportunity to meet someone new today, and it could happen in the most unexpected way. The rest of you can enjoy sporting activities or anything that you do with friends in a group or a social setting. Therefore, 'phone your friends and suggest a game of golf or something similar.

Saturday, 17th May
Venus trine Uranus

A day of passionate intensity is indicated by the aspect from Venus to Uranus! Lock the doors, take the 'phone off the hook and settle down to some serious amorous entanglement with your lover.

Sunday, 18th May
Moon trine Venus

Take the opportunity to show your loved ones how much you care today, and if you accompany your remarks with a gift of flowers or chocolates, so much the better. All this will be well received and much appreciated by your loved one. This spin-off may be a wonderful revival of your sex life. Well, it's worth a try, isn't it?

Monday, 19th May
Moon trine Jupiter

There will be a couple of lucky breaks that help you sort out a number of sticky family or relationship problems that have been bugging you. Help will come from hidden or unexpected sources and you'll be on the receiving end of more kindness than you can usually expect from the world around you. Older female relatives will come to your aid by helping out in a practical way or by soothing the family's feelings.

Tuesday, 20th May
Sun trine Neptune

You seem to be in a dreamy mood and any conversation that you have with friends and colleagues will tend to be on the subject of dreams, secret desires and the nature of love. How fascinating!

Wednesday, 21st May
Sun into Gemini

Today the Sun enters your solar eighth house of beginnings and endings. Thus, over the next month, you can expect something to wind its way to a conclusion, while something else starts to take its place. This doesn't seem to signify a major benchmark or any really big event in your life, but it does mark one of those small turning points that we all go through from time to time.

Thursday, 22nd May
Full Moon

Today's Full Moon seems to be highlighting a minor problem in connection with financial matters. You may have been overspending recently and this could be the cause of your current financial embarrassment, but there does seem to be something deeper to be considered here. Perhaps the firm you work for has a temporary problem, or maybe your partner is a bit short of cash just now?

Friday, 23rd May
Venus sextile Saturn

There is an opportunity to set something in motion today which should stand the test of time. This may be the start of a new personal relationship or it may be a working arrangement of some kind. The chances are that your 'partner' will be an older man, or a woman who is in a position of authority. You must also keep an eye on other people's finances now, for example by following the progress of any organisation that you work for or supply with goods or services.

Saturday, 24th May
Sun opposite Pluto

You are still being plagued with joint financial problems. It may be a good idea to review the way you and your partner deal with money and then work out what to do for the best. You may have a business partner who is not dealing fairly with you, and it is equally possible that you are not dealing quite fairly with others.

Sunday, 25th May
Moon square Saturn

You may feel somewhat under the weather today, and the possibilities range from bruising a bone or a joint or going down with a cold. Even if there is nothing more than a sense of fatigue, you could be feeling quite under par. Try to rest and relax as much as you can.

Monday, 26th May
Moon conjunct Neptune

Your mind seems to be full of quite inspired ideas, but are they really practical? It may be better to leave anything that is detailed, difficult or terribly important until your brain is a little less full of fluff!

Tuesday, 27th May
Venus trine Jupiter

You can afford to indulge yourself, either by enjoying a long, languid lie in a softly-scented bubble bath or by treating yourself and your loved ones to a special meal and a great night out. This is a wonderful time for purchasing luxury items for the home as well. In short, forget that you are one of the world's workers for once, and live like a king for a day!

Wednesday, 28th May
Venus square Mars

You're likely to be swept off your feet by a new attraction today. Someone you meet in a social setting could give you palpitations, and this could be the start of a passionate whirlwind romance. Of course, he or she may not really be your true soul mate since the attraction seems to be totally sexual in nature. However, you'll both have fun finding out. Passions of all sorts run high at the moment, so you could also expect an explosion of jealousy amongst your friends.

Thursday, 29th May
Sun trine Uranus

Financially, today's events should be very beneficial. Some will receive a windfall, while others could benefit from an insurance or endowment policy. Whatever the reason, you

may as well have an impromptu celebration at home to
mark the occasion.

Friday, 30th May
Moon square Venus

There's an intimate feel to today's stars as the Moon and
Venus are in aspect in the romantic and sexual areas of
your horoscope. This could herald a passionate embrace
which, if not wise is certainly enjoyable. In financial affairs,
try not to overspend on pleasure.

Saturday, 31st May
Moon sextile Uranus

A friend may come up with a solution to some of your
problems. He or she will suggest easier ways of doing
things either at home or at work, and these ideas could be
quite imaginative or even revolutionary way. Welcome
their input, because you are simply too close to the
situation to be able to see it clearly.

June at a Glance

LOVE	♥	♥			
WORK	★	★			
MONEY	$	$	$		
FITNESS	🌀	🌀	🌀		
LUCK	U	U	U	U	

Sunday, 1st June
Moon sextile Jupiter

An unexpected stroke of luck could bring you a bit more money than you had bargained for, and this is most likely to come as the result of a job you completed some time ago. You may even have half-forgotten it all, only to find that something is still accruing from it.

Monday, 2nd June
Moon square Uranus

This is an uneasy day for all relationship matters. You may want a happy and harmonious partnership, only to find that your lover is tense and tetchy and inclined to misunderstand (probably quite deliberately), everything that you do. Alternatively, you may both want to be happy together, only to find that the fates are intervening and contriving to keep you apart.

Tuesday, 3rd June
Moon conjunct Mercury

Spend today in the company of someone you love. You need some emotional reassurance and can only get it by an affectionate heart-to-heart. The beginning of any sort of partnership, romantic or business, is strongly favoured today.

Wednesday, 4th June
Venus into Cancer

Venus enters your solar ninth house of exploration this month and this may make you slightly restless. Venus is concerned with the pleasures of life and also with leisure activities of all kinds, so explore such ideas as your sporting interests, or perhaps listening to interesting music or going to art galleries and the like. You may want to travel somewhere new and interesting soon.

Thursday, 5th June
New Moon

Apart from a New Moon today, there are no major planetary happenings. This suggests that you avoid making major changes in your life just now but make a couple of fresh starts in very minor matters. You may feel like taking your partner to task over their irritating ways, but perhaps today is not the best day for doing this.

Friday, 6th June
Mercury trine Mars

A stimulating conversation will prove to you that your little grey cells are in fine working order. Sluggish thinking processes are banished as Mercury aspects Mars to fill your time with heady debates and enjoyable arguments.

Saturday, 7th June
Sun sextile Saturn

This is a great day for business partnerships. You and your colleagues should be able to conclude something that you have been working on or you may start a new project now. Either way, lady luck is with you. If you decide to start a venture with new people, this will work well too.

Sunday, 8th June
Mercury into Gemini

Mercury moves into one of the most sensitive areas of your chart from today. Anything of an intimate nature, from your physical relationships to the state of your bank balance, comes under scrutiny now. Turn your heightened perceptions to your love life, important partnerships, and any affair that deals with investment, insurance, tax or shared resources. An intelligent approach now will save you a lot of problems later.

Monday, 9th June
Mercury trine Neptune

A phone call or letter should bring good news about money today. In fact, the news could be so good that it will leave you rather bemused and uncertain about what to do next. Don't worry, you'll sort it all out in time.

Tuesday, 10th June
Jupiter retrograde

Jupiter turns to retrograde motion today and it will continue to move backwards in your chart for a few weeks to come. This will bring a slowing down in all domestic and family matters and it may also bring more expense in these areas than you had anticipated.

Wednesday, 11th June
Sun trine Jupiter

Your partner, your close associates and your closest allies will see eye-to-eye with you today and they may even be on hand to help you out of a domestic crisis or two. You will probably buy some kind of new item for the home now, and you will have to ask another family member to help you put it exactly where you want it to be.

Thursday, 12th June
Mercury trine Uranus

The eloquence with which you communicate your ideas is staggering now. Things you feel strongly about can be argued in a persuasive and winning manner. On the subjects of domestic issues and family concerns, a revolutionary approach will win approval from those closest to you. Forget the tried and true because the combination of Mercury and Uranus shows that innovation is the key to understanding. Younger family members will respond to your non-traditional stance.

Friday, 13th June
Moon conjunct Mars

Your ideals verge on the revolutionary as the Moon links up with Mars in your house of dreams and aspirations. Not for you quietly mulling over the injustices of this world, you'll want to man the barricades to do something about it. Even if your aspirations don't reach as high as changing the whole world, you'll still have a few tall orders to accomplish. Your anger is likely to be directed at the 'system' now, but some friends could come in for a little flack too.

Saturday, 14th June
Moon trine Uranus

You can expect the unexpected in the domestic sphere of your life today. Friends may drop in unannounced and a family member may bring home a gift or a treat just for you. A loan may be repaid, and any favours that you have done to others can also be returned to you now. Your intuition will guide you strongly today and there may be some kind of inner voice which keeps you from saying or doing the wrong thing.

Sunday, 15th June
Mars trine Neptune

The positive aspect between Mars and Neptune will make you aware of an ideal or a worthy cause that you'd like to be involved in. You'll be moved by the plight of those less fortunate than yourself and will wish to do something concrete to help. You're convinced that a better world is possible and will be determined to do your bit. Perhaps you could turn your energies to organising a successful fund-raising event?

Monday, 16th June
Moon square Neptune

Though you would prefer a little solitude today, someone will force their presence on you. Even though you won't like to be rude, it might be best to ask them to back off because the effect of any disruption to your routine could offend your delicate sensibilities.

Tuesday, 17th June
Moon trine Venus

The ideal situation for you is to be relaxed in a shaded bar sipping a cocktail, or stretched out on some exotic shore complete with gently swaying palm trees and a beautiful blue sea. Does that sound good? You could do with a much-needed break, but if you're still stuck in the daily drudgery you can always dream. Perhaps you should do more than that and book a holiday now.

Wednesday, 18th June
Mercury sextile Saturn

There seems to be news of something good that is about to occur in your place of work. This could reflect an improving financial situation in the firm or organisation that you work for and, if so, this will ultimately be good for you too.

Thursday, 19th June
Mars into Libra

The planet of energy, Mars, moves into the most private area of your chart now showing that unconsidered actions are not the way forward. It's time to sit back, think things through and work out a good strategy for future progress. If your career affairs have been a battlefield of petty politics and in-fighting, then it's your chance to win the upper hand by outflanking the opposition. In more personal affairs too, the strategic influence of Mars gives the impetus to develop subtle tactics to win the object of your desire.

Friday, 20th June
Full Moon

If you've been sensible with your cash, today's Full Moon shows that there are certain monetary strictures that may no longer be needed. Areas in which you've been lax need attention too, for spendthrift tendencies may require corrective measures. This is a time to sort out your fiscal state to the best advantage. Like a plant, some judicious pruning and encouraging will do your bank balance a lot of good.

Saturday, 21st June
Sun into Cancer

The Sun moves into your solar ninth house today and it will stay there for a month. This is a good time to travel overseas or to explore new neighbourhoods, and also to take an interest in spiritual matters. You may find yourself keen to read about religious or philosophical subjects or even to explore the world of psychic healing over the next month or so.

Sunday, 22nd June
Sun square Mars

Think before you act, that's the astral message today! Any impulsive actions made at this time will be regretted, so take care. Breathe deeply and count to ten before you commit yourself to anything!

Monday, 23rd June
Mercury into Cancer

Mercury enters your solar house of adventure and philosophy from today to stimulate your curiosity.

Everything from international affairs to religious questions will tax your mind. Your desire to travel will be boosted for a few weeks, as indeed will a need to expand your knowledge, perhaps by taking up a course at a local college. Keep an open mind. Allow yourself encounters with new ideas.

Tuesday, 24th June
Mercury square Mars

Be careful when operating machinery today, especially if you use any of this directly or indirectly for travelling purposes. It's best to double-check any equipment that is mobile or portable before using it now.

Wednesday, 25th June
Sun conjunct Mercury

If you have any kind of legal or official matter to deal with, this is a good day to get on with it. It is a good time to sign contracts or agreements or to make a business deal. You seem to be taking a deep interest in spiritual matters now and this may be the start of something which will affect the course of your life from now on.

Thursday, 26th June
Mars sextile Pluto

Strategy and financial planning are the favoured activities for today. You need to think about your financial situation and assess your income and outgoings. You'll probably find that there are better rates of interest to be had for loans, and various small debts with which you can dispense.

Friday, 27th June
Venus opposite Neptune

The poetic, dreamy side of your emotional nature is in

evidence today as Venus and Neptune take you on a joyride filled with fantasy. Your visionary abilities show you the possibilities that await. Incurably romantic and artistically gifted, there seems no end to the things you could achieve . . . if only you could get around to it. You're no fool and know deep down that inspiration without hard work is a waste of time. Enjoy this period, but don't forget that effort is required to make all dreams come true.

Saturday, 28th June
Venus into Leo

Venus moves into your solar house of ambition and prominence from today. If you're involved in any career in the arts, beautification, entertainment or public relations, then you're bound to do well over the next few weeks. Those who work for women bosses won't do badly either since a female influence in the workplace will aid your ambitions. Since Venus is the planet of charisma, use diplomacy to solve professional problems. You can hardly fail to win with such a capacity for charm.

Sunday, 29th June
Moon square Venus

A woman may be a bit of a pain in the neck to you today and your relationships with women in general seem to be less than good. Partnerships of all kinds will need a bit of extra effort to make them work now, and you may find that your other half is a bit downhearted or irritable now. It may be hard to influence those who matter or to make an impression on authority figures.

Monday, 30th June
Moon sextile Mercury

If you suggest a holiday or an unusual trip to your partner today, you will be delighted by his or her response. Any ideas that you talk over with others now will be well received, even if they are rather new and revolutionary. If you have any kind of legal or official matters on your mind, these too will begin to work in the way you want. Even outright enemies will lay off for a while.

July at a Glance

LOVE	♥				
WORK	★	★			
MONEY	$				
FITNESS	⧬	⧬			
LUCK	∪	∪	∪	∪	∪

Tuesday, 1st July
Venus trine Pluto

A woman may be instrumental in helping you solve a money or business problem of some kind. This woman may not be a specialist in your own particular sphere, but her sound, common-sense ideas will help you to see your situation more clearly. If you do decide to consult a financial specialist, you will get some useful advice now.

Wednesday, 2nd July
Mercury square Saturn

Whatever you try to say will be wrong today. You may try to tackle someone who is in a position of authority, only to find that they walk all over you. You may not feel on top form health-wise, so try to rest as much as you can.

However bad things are, remember that the planets always move on and that in astrology, as in life, there are good times and bad times.

Thursday, 3rd July
Venus sextile Mars

Though inwardly you may be seething, you can still get your own way in professional affairs if you are charming. You may have a smile like a crocodile today, but that's all to the good. If colleagues have been false to you, then it's okay to be false in return. If an employer is too eager to throw his weight about, direct opposition could work against you, so smile ... and bide your time! How could we teach you anything about cunning?

Friday, 4th July
New Moon

The New Moon in your house of adventure urges you to push ahead with new projects. You're in a self-confident mood, and feel able to tackle anything the world throws at you. There's a lure of the exotic today as well, as far-off places exert a powerful attraction. Think again about widening your personal horizons, by travel or by taking up an educational course. Intellectually you're on top form and your curiosity is boundless.

Saturday, 5th July
Venus opposite Uranus

When an ill wind blows it does no one any good, and today's ill wind, although distressing for someone else, may be just the opportunity that you have been looking for. A colleague's fall from grace may be a stepping stone to achievement for you.

Sunday, 6th July
Mars trine Uranus

There's no point in charging in and trying to organise everyone else today. You need to be calm, think things through and work out the best moves, just as if you were playing chess. Good opportunities are coming up, but it's up to you how best you use them.

Monday, 7th July
Mercury opposite Neptune

This is not the ideal day for travel of any kind but, if you must travel, then allow extra time for delays. You may find that any journey that you take now disappoints or frustrates you. Even a simple shopping expedition will irritate you now.

Tuesday, 8th July
Mercury into Leo

There's a certain flexibility entering your career structure as indicated by the presence of Mercury in your solar area of ambition from today. You can now turn your acute mind to all sorts of career problems and solve them to everyone's satisfaction, and your own personal advantage. Your powers of persuasion will be heightened from now on, ensuring that you charm bosses and employers to get your own way. Those seeking work should attend interviews, because you'll shine!

Wednesday, 9th July
Mercury trine Pluto

If you are trying to raise money for a business venture or an enterprise of any kind, today should be a good day to do it. You may have to take others into your confidence now, but the chances are that they will help you rather than take advantage of your openness.

Thursday, 10th July
Moon trine Neptune

A good day for your social life when you can enjoy yourself in the company of like-minded people who appreciate your finer qualities. A journey in the company of friends will be marvellous.

Friday, 11th July
Sun square Saturn

You long to be sitting in a low-slung convertible, with the top down and the wind blowing through your long tawny locks. (So, blokes can have long tawny locks too!) You long for freedom, for the perfect romance and the chance to be yourself for once. However, the reality is that the chores keep on piling up around you and that life is full of boring responsibilities.

Saturday, 12th July
Moon sextile Venus

This is a good time to go out looking for gifts for others. Take a look around and see if you can do a bit of bargain-hunting so that you can save time, shoe-leather and money later in the year. This is a good time to buy yourself a few small luxuries.

Sunday, 13th July
Moon square Neptune

Take care Scorpio, because today you'll be so impressionable that someone unscrupulous could tell you that black is white, and you'll believe them. Try to keep your tongue in check and don't believe any gossip!

Monday, 14th July
Jupiter sextile Saturn

Nothing worth having is ever easy, but today you'll realise

that with just a little more effort you can gain your heart's desire without breaking either the bank or your neck. Everything is possible at this very hopeful time.

Tuesday, 15th July
Mercury sextile Mars

Though there may be problems at work you can defeat all opposition with a little forethought. The shrewdness of Mercury unites with the strategic cunning of Mars to enable you to run rings around any opponent.

Wednesday, 16th July
Moon sextile Uranus

There should be a sudden and unexpected windfall for you or a relative. What seems certain is that if such a windfall does arrive, you will spend it on household goods that will benefit all the family – but don't forget to treat yourself as well. You may feel like breaking out of a rut and having a bit of freedom now, but you are actually more likely to spend any free time loafing around your home.

Thursday, 17th July
Moon trine Saturn

An excellent aspect between the Moon and Saturn suggests that anything to do with parents or parental figures will be successful today. If you visit your parents, you will enjoy their company and if you need any help from them, they will be only too happy to oblige.

Friday, 18th July
Mercury opposite Jupiter

You won't get much sense out of anyone today, and nobody will understand what you are trying to achieve. You may be keen to prove a point only to find that others have a completely different perspective, and that they are unwilling to listen to what you have to say. A youngish man may prove to be particularly obtuse now.

Saturday, 19th July
Moon square Saturn

A disturbing thought could put you off your work today or even make you feel ill, but be that as it may, a troublesome reality must be faced – even if you find the going hard. At least you're determined enough to make the best of it.

Sunday, 20th July
Full Moon

This is likely to be a really awkward day for any kind of travelling. A vehicle could let you down just when you most need it or the public transport that you usually rely upon could suddenly disappear from the face of the earth.

Monday, 21st July
Sun opposite Neptune

'Am I doing the right thing?' That's the question buzzing around your head today as confusion and doubt sets in. It's all the fault of the solar opposition to Neptune which has you questioning ideas and aims that you've taken for granted for so long. If you're feeling at all discouraged by the sheer volume of the tasks ahead, you should console yourself with the thought that even Rome wasn't built in a day. Time and determination will solve this problem, and once this aspect is past your true aims will again be evident.

Tuesday, 22nd July
Sun into Leo

The Sun moves decisively into your horoscopic area of ambition from today, bringing a month when your worldly progress will achieve absolute priority. You need to feel that what you are doing is worthwhile and has more meaning than simply paying the bills. You may feel the urge to change you career, to make a long-term commitment to a worthwhile cause, or simply to demand recognition for past efforts. However this ambitious phase is manifested, you can be sure that your prospects are considerably boosted from now on.

Wednesday, 23rd July
Venus into Virgo

Venus moves into your eleventh house of friendship and group activities today, bringing a few weeks of happiness and harmony for you and your friends. You could fall in love under this transit or you could reaffirm your feelings towards a current partner. You should be looking and feeling rather good now but if not, this is a good time to spend some money on your appearance and also to do something about any nagging health problems.

Thursday, 24th July
Moon trine Pluto

You will find a way to successfully transform some element of your job. You will also find a way of earning more money now, even though it may be a while before you see the results of all your efforts.

Friday, 25th July
Venus square Pluto

Alhough your desires incline to extravagant fun, the financial realities won't permit you to spend, spend, spend. A female friend who may be a bad influence could leave your life at this time.

Saturday, 26th July
Mars trine Jupiter

You seem to be on the point of changing your mind about a number of things just now. You may decide that the group of people with whom you have been associating are becoming increasingly childish, boring or even dangerous to be with. If so, face up to the fact that your ideals are different from theirs and leave them to get on with life without you.

Sunday, 27th July
Mercury into Virgo

The swift-moving planet, Mercury, enters your eleventh solar house today and gives a remarkable uplift to your social prospects. During the next few weeks you'll find yourself at the centre of friendly interactions. People will seek you out for the pleasure of your company. It's also a good time to get in contact with distant friends and those you haven't seen for a while. The only fly in the ointment is that you shouldn't expect a small 'phone bill.

Monday, 28th July
Mars opposite Saturn

This could be a pretty frustrating day with you trying to make headway at work, with everyone else around you on go-slow. You may have impetus but it's certain that they won't, so you may have to go at the pace of the slowest colleague, which won't do your blood pressure any good at all.

Tuesday, 29th July
Sun opposite Uranus

There will be setbacks to your plans today and a number of things may go suddenly and inexplicably wrong. Murphy's Law is in operation now, so don't expect to get very far with anything at the moment. You may have to spend time mending or replacing things that have been accidentally broken.

Wednesday, 30th July
Moon trine Mars

You could be in for a strangely erotic interlude or a really unforgettable sexual experience. You may make love in strange places or with strange people. Everyone experiments a bit from time to time but, as with all sexual matters, take care of yourself. However, you may use these odd planetary energies to investigate the paranormal instead.

Thursday, 31st July
Moon sextile Mercury

You're terribly restless today and can't wait to get away from the jaded and familiar. Though your basic inclinations may be to travel as far away as you can, you'd be the first to admit that it's not always possible. If you are chained to the domestic or work scene then you need something to take your mind off the usual affairs of life. A good conversation, a fascinating book or an absorbing television show should improve your mood.

August at a Glance

LOVE	♥	♥	♥		
WORK	★	★	★	★	
MONEY	$	$	$		
FITNESS	〰	〰	〰		
LUCK	∪	∪			

Friday, 1st August
Saturn retrograde

You will have to keep a close eye on health matters over the next few weeks, because Saturn will not be well placed in the health area of your chart. You may have thought you had got over some kind of illness, or you may have thought that a chronic situation was in abeyance. Well, that may be the case in a few months' time, but for the time being, you will have to take care.

Saturday, 2nd August
Moon trine Pluto

You can make slow and subtle moves towards success in your career today. It is not a good time to be open about your plans; go about things slowly and quietly, until the time comes to speak out. Luck is with you in connection with money now too and something that has been held up in the works may come through now.

Sunday, 3rd August
New Moon

Take it as easily as you can today, stick more or less to

your usual routine and, if you do try something new, make sure that it is nothing large or important. A woman may be instrumental in helping you achieve an ambition today and you should be grateful to her for her efforts on your behalf.

Monday, 4th August
Moon sextile Mars

Ladies who happen to be reading this can expect a rather pleasant flirtation with a nice man at your place of work. Even if you don't work, you may enjoy a pleasant telephone flirtation with a tradesman or similar! Those of you who have social or career-based ambitions will have a very good day today, because your status among your colleagues and in your community is about to be enhanced.

Tuesday, 5th August
Moon conjunct Mercury

It's a good day to get in touch with friends that you haven't seen in ages, so keep some blank spaces in your diary for a few select social events this week; it's good to talk things over with some special people in your life. You're in a thoughtful frame of mind for much of the time, but it's an excellent idea to get another perspective on your plans.

Wednesday, 6th August
Moon conjunct Venus

If you are asked to join in any kind of group activity today, then do so because you will get much more out of this than you had bargained for. You will make new friends and be filled with new and exciting ideas. It is possible that you will begin to realise that someone whom you had hitherto considered to be nothing more than a friend is rapidly turning into someone special.

Thursday, 7th August
Moon sextile Pluto

Something that you lost or mislaid could come to light now. Favours that you have done for others, such as a loan, may be repaid On the other hand, you may want to clear any debts that you owe others. There is some good news about money mattes but it may be a while before the cash materialises.

Friday, 8th August
Moon sextile Sun

Your mood is calm and you seem content to go along with what others want today. Fortunately, others seem to want much the same as you do, so there shouldn't be any conflict of interest now.

Saturday, 9th August
Sun opposite Jupiter

You may need to be at work extra early just when your arrangements for delivering your children to school have collapsed. You could have to stay indoors waiting for something to be delivered or mended, just when you absolutely must be at work. In short, the demands of work and home are incompatible today and you will feel the full pressure of both.

Sunday, 10th August
Mars square Neptune

You might be feeling rather powerless today because the harsh aspect between Mars and Neptune saps your confidence and makes you pretty indecisive. Leave any important documents and decisions to another day.

Monday, 11th August
Moon square Sun

A world-weary mood takes a hold under a harsh lunar aspect to the Sun today. You've put up with a lot of pressures recently, and even though the more general outlook is good you are showing the strain. The expectations others have of you is a major factor. You've done a lot for others recently, but you could really do with a day off.

Tuesday, 12th August
Sun trine Saturn

Your mind is more firmly fixed on the main chance today and you'll have a clearer view of your goals. You seem to be putting a lot of thought into both your personal, domestic needs and also your worldly ambitions. An older or more experienced person could be of great help to you now, by showing you how to obtain the knowledge and experience you need in your line of work.

Wednesday, 13th August
Pluto direct

After a long period of retrograde movement Pluto now moves into direct motion. This is a distant and very slow-moving planet and its effects tend to last a long time. For example, Mercury moves backwards three times a year for two-to-three weeks each time, while Pluto can spend a third of a year in retrograde motion. This forward movement in your solar second house of money and possessions will make it easier for you to sort out or to improve your financial position.

Thursday, 14th August
Mars into Scorpio

This is the start of an active and dynamic period, for Mars

moves into your own sign, endowing you with considerable energy and drive. There's no problem with confidence any more since, if anything, Mars makes you more assertive than ever. The only warning note is that you'll tend to be quite hasty, so try to slow down while driving or operating any machinery. This speedy feel to the planet also makes minor accidents likely, so be on your guard.

Friday, 15th August
Venus trine Neptune

Today shows what an inspired and indeed inspiring person you can be. The splendid aspect of Venus and Neptune brings the true poetry in your soul into the full light of day. Artistically you can show that you have gifts that no one suspected. You could even surprise yourself! You may be attracted to painting, music and poetry to express your vision. Original insights combined with talent are the order of the day.

Saturday, 16th August
Venus into Libra

As Venus enters your solar house of secrets and psychology, it's obvious that the next few weeks will increase the importance of discretion in your romantic life. You'll find that it'll be wise to draw a veil over the more intimate side of your nature, and you'll be less inclined to confide your deepest secrets even to your closest friends. Quiet interludes with the one you love will be far more attractive than painting the town red just now.

Sunday, 17th August
Mercury retrograde

Today begins a period when your optimism will fall short of its usual level, which is the fault of Mercury turning retrograde. This isn't a serious problem, but you must be aware that at times you will feel as if your hopes have been dashed and your faith in friends misplaced. Of course there's little substance in these feelings, yet rumours in the next few weeks may be disturbing.

Monday, 18th August
Full Moon

The Full Moon today focuses firmly on family and domestic issues. Perhaps it's time for some straight talking, because this is the best opportunity you'll get to put an end to home-based or emotional problems. In some ways it's time to put your cards on the table, yet equally to give credit and take some share of blame in family affairs. Apart from such personal concerns it's also favourble to speak to someone in authority about your ambitions. .

Tuesday, 19th August
Moon opposite Mercury

Your mind may be set on having fun with your friends, but try not to overload your already stretched schedule. Practical affairs have to be dealt with whether you're in the mood or not. I know you want to party, but you'll only end up over-tired and edgy. It may be a case of all work and no play, but it's better in the long run. Resist friends who insist that you be sociable. That's only replacing one duty with another.

Wednesday, 20th August
Moon sextile Neptune

If ever there was a day for a cuddle on the sofa then this is it. You're sentimental, sensitive and extremely sensuous, so time spent with a lover should be fun. However, if there isn't a lover on offer, a weepy film or a romantic novel will just have to do!

Thursday, 21st August
Venus trine Uranus

You seem to have a stroke of genius today that helps you to either get a creative project on the right lines or to sort out some kind of domestic dispute, or both. A woman will be very helpful, possibly coming up with just the right idea at the right moment. Home is where the heart is today, so stay close to the kitchen and the hearth with your lover and keep the rest of the world at a distance.

Friday, 22nd August
Mars square Uranus

Female readers are in danger of taking a man's blandishments far too seriously. So he says you have lovely eyes, so what? This doesn't mean that he is going to love you forever, does it? He may appear to be unbearably attracted to you but is this attraction likely to last after you have given him your all? Possibly not. Don't take anything or anyone seriously today.

Saturday, 23rd August
Sun into Virgo

As the Sun makes its yearly entrance into your eleventh solar house, you can be sure that friends and acquaintances are going to have a powerful influence on your prospects. The Sun's harmonious angle gives you optimism and vitality. Social life will increase in importance over the next month, and you'll be a popular and much sought-after person. Obstacles that have irritated you will now be swept clean away.

Sunday, 24th August
Moon trine Neptune

You and a close friend or partner will be totally in tune with each other today. Communication becomes almost instinctive as you both experience an intimacy that is akin to telepathy.

Monday, 25th August
Sun square Pluto

You seem to be looking for a change of pace now with less emphasis on materialism and more on friendship, plus a better quality of life. You also seem keen to educate yourself in some way.

Tuesday, 26th August
Moon sextile Saturn

No one could beat you in the common-sense stakes today. You'll be shrewd, careful and extremely insightful when it comes to all matters concerning work and money.

Wednesday, 27th August
Moon sextile Sun

This is a great day for getting out and about, meeting up with friends and attending social gatherings of all kinds. You should have a pretty good time in company because this is not a day for solitary activity.

Thursday, 28th August
Venus trine Jupiter

It would be just as well to sit down, look around your home and think about what you want to do with it. Before buying, selling, renovating or decorating anything that you possess, you must take the time and the trouble to consider how your life is likely to go over the next few years and then work out the most reasonable and sensible way to manage things.

Friday, 29th August
Mercury sextile Mars

This is a great day for having fun and for temporarily shelving all those boring and trying responsibilities. You may feel in a kind of 'breakout' mood in which you leave your normal routine behind and spend the day doing things that are new and unusual. Your mind will be buzzing with new ideas and you may profitably spend a good part of the day discussing these with colleagues or friends.

Saturday, 30th August
Moon square Mars

You're no stranger to opposition; in fact, sometimes it seems that obstacles are thrown in your path constantly! On the other hand, you do tend to get your own way when you put your mind to it. There's that determined look in your eye today, so I doubt that anyone will put up more than half-hearted resistance to your plans!

Sunday, 31st August
Sun conjunct Mercury

The conjunction of the Sun and Mercury makes this one of the most exciting days of the year. Mentally you are on top form, and communications of all kinds will work to your benefit. You can't let others make all the running now, so get out and about and circulate. You'll find that friends, colleagues and supporters will all help you make your dreams come true. You have the heaven-sent ability to be in the right place at the right time and, more importantly, to say the right things!

September at a Glance

LOVE	♥	♥	♥		
WORK	★	★	★	★	★
MONEY	$	$	$	$	$
FITNESS	🔊	🔊	🔊		
LUCK	U	U	U		

Monday, 1st September
New Moon eclipse

Today's lunar eclipse may make you feel uncomfortable around people. Perhaps you are painfully aware of your character defects or supposed inferiorities. Nothing could be further from the truth, since you come over as a capable and amusing companion. Try to shake off any feelings of negativity. If you are truly concerned when comparing yourself to new acquaintances, remember that they're bound to have faults too.

Tuesday, 2nd September
Venus opposite Saturn

There seems to be a clash between what you want and what you get today. What you would like to do is to snooze in a hammock under a tree with a book, a glass of something cool and restorative nearby and an exciting young lover about to visit at any moment. What you get is a lot of work, the boss chasing you from pillar to post and the kids coming home with their sports clothes all filthy and needing to be washed and ironed by tomorrow morning.

Wednesday, 3rd September
Moon trine Neptune

A great time to get out and about, to enjoy the company of friends and to travel somewhere new. Any novel location you end up in will be exactly to your taste, as indeed will any new person that you meet there.

Thursday, 4th September
Moon trine Jupiter

Other people will ask for your help today and you will be only too happy to give them a hand, especially if you are returning past favours. This is a good time to return anything that you have borrowed, to put in a deserved good word for someone or to cheer up a downhearted friend.

Friday, 5th September
Moon conjunct Venus

You really are a soft touch today, and so much so that you must avoid being taken for a ride by others. The people you help may be trying it on in some way, perhaps trying to shift the responsibility for living their lives or paying their debts on to you. A friend may whisper secrets into your ear and you will have to respect their confidence.

Saturday, 6th September
Sun sextile Mars

The emphasis today will be on your social life rather than home affairs or your work. Friends may take you off to some kind of local entertainment, or you may be invited to an unexpectedly good party. This is a wonderful day for romance, especially for our female readers. You may also enjoy sporting activities in the company of friends.

Sunday, 7th September
Mercury square Pluto

You could suffer from a financial hitch over the next couple of days. This is because you are being made aware that you need to think about your finances and to do something about them. It is no good being the last of the big spenders, or you'll soon be broke! Start to save something for a rainy day from now on.

Monday, 8th September
Moon sextile Neptune

If you feel that something is right and that there have been too many issues brushed under the carpet, then speak up because you will receive a fair hearing today. Your refined sensitivities could help you address the sometimes difficult issues involved.

Tuesday, 9th September
Moon sextile Jupiter

Money-wise and in dealings with authority you're in luck today. A marvellous astral combination ensures that you won't take the less-than-perfect, and you are forceful and assertive. Just make sure that you don't take this wilfulness too far, otherwise you could end up dishing out far more than anyone deserves. At least you are going to get what you want.

Wednesday, 10th September
Mercury direct

If you've not been seeing eye-to-eye with certain friends recently, you can put the blame on Mercury's wayward course which has made all social relations much more difficult recently. Fortunately, the tiny planet is now moving along the right road so it's time to pour oil on troubled waters and re-establish the friendly social links you previously enjoyed.

Thursday, 11th September
Venus square Neptune

Though you aren't usually timid, you'll shy away from the slightest hint of conflict today. The negative aspect between Venus and Neptune makes you ultra-sensitive with a delicate ego. You're likely to crumble in the face of any criticism, no matter how constructive it could be at other times. The best bet is to retreat into a haven of seclusion. You're too tender to risk the insensitivity of others today.

Friday, 12th September
Venus into Scorpio

The luxury-loving planet, Venus, is suggesting that this is a great time to spoil yourself and also to enjoy yourself. So treat yourself to something nice and new for you alone. A new outfit would be a good idea, or a few nice-smelling toiletries. Throw a party for your favourite friends and don't look the other way if there's someone who seems to be fancying you.

Saturday, 13th September
Moon conjunct Uranus

You may decide to move house! Although this may look like a spur-of-the-moment decision, it has probably been lurking at the back of your mind for a long time but you may not have felt like talking to others about it. Another possibility is that you decide to alter your present home in some dramatic way. At the very least, you could buy a large household item.

Sunday, 14th September
Moon square Mars

Some days it's hard to please anybody, including yourself. No sooner do you decide on a course of action than you run into all sorts of objections and criticisms from your family. You'll feel that they should really trust your judgement by now, and you will be inclined to add fuel to the fire by coming back with a few criticisms of your own. Don't be paranoid! Ignore all this carping and just get on with what you want to do. Everyone else is bound to fall into line later.

Monday, 15th September
Mercury sextile Venus

It's rare that Mercury and Venus get far enough apart to make an angle to each other, but that's the case today. This astral event heralds a boost to your social life, your capacity to make new friends and your personal charm. What more do you need?

Tuesday, 16th September
Full Moon eclipse

Today's eclipse casts a shadow over your sense of fun and frivolity. Life may seem too serious to be bothered with flippant activities or people. A serious attitude will prevail, but that shouldn't get you down. Nothing has really changed so your mood should soon lighten up.

Wednesday, 17th September
Venus square Uranus

You may feel ground down by family demands and domestic problems today. You may desperately need to get out to work, only to be stuck at home waiting for the plumber or some other specialist tradesperson. An older female may set out to upset you, or, she may act in such an unpredictable and eccentric manner that you simply won't know what to do for the best.

Thursday, 18th September
Moon conjunct Saturn

It's not a day for frivolity in any shape or form! The Moon is in conjunction with Saturn showing that it's time to roll up your sleeves and get down to some hard graft. You've got such a capacity for productive effort it would be a pity to waste it.

Friday, 19th September
Sun trine Neptune

A short holiday could bring you far more than you expected because you could find yourself being swept off your feet by a bright and humorous lover. You will soon be faced with a major decision about your special relationship, which could herald the end of a casual relationship and the start of something much deeper and important. Your hopes and dreams should soon start to be realised.

Saturday, 20th September
Moon opposite Mars

If your other half has got any ideas of chaining you to the kitchen sink, then someone is in for a surprise. You're in no mood to pander to the desires of anyone other than yourself, so any attempt to make you toe the line will result in a furious outburst. You're a positive dynamo of energy today and should seek some more constructive way of burning off the excess. Otherwise your close relationships could resemble a medium-sized war by this evening.

Sunday, 21st September
Moon opposite Pluto

Guard against being manipulated by others or agreeing to take responsibility for anything when you are not in possession of the full facts. Be on guard against those who want to manipulate you for their own ends either in connection with money or a relationship matter.

Monday, 22nd September
Sun into Libra

The Sun moves into your house of secrets and psychology today, making you very aware of your own inner world of dreams and imagination. For the next month you'll sense the hurdles that face you, and all those things that tend to restrict your freedom. However, your imagination and almost psychic insight will provide the necessary clues to overcome these obstacles. Issues of privacy are very important over the next few weeks.

Tuesday, 23rd September
Venus square Jupiter

If you go out to the shops today, watch what you spend because this isn't the time to acquire goods for yourself or your home. It is be better to keep any extra cash that you have safely tucked away in case of urgent repairs or repayment of debts. There isn't much chance of money coming in to you just now either.

Wednesday, 24th September
Mars sextile Neptune

A brilliant and innovative idea should be acted upon immediately. Don't doubt your own inspiration, because your unconscious mind is giving you a message that should not be ignored. A journey to the sea or any large body of water will help your mental processes.

Thursday, 25th September
Moon opposite Neptune

I'm afraid that you're in rather a confused state of mind today. You may know what you mean, yet no one else will. Your feelings and intuitions are very strong now, but when it comes to putting your insights into words, you're at a loss. Arguments of any kind, whether friendly or aggressive will send you fleeing to the hills, since you can't stand any disharmony in your delicate state.

Friday, 26th September
Sun sextile Pluto

You seem to be on an inward journey today. Maybe you need to work out what your true values are and how they match up with those of the people who are around you. If there is a choice between doing something dishonest for short-term gains or doing without the goodies in order to remain honest, decent and true to yourself, you know you will make the right decision.

Saturday, 27th September
Sun trine Uranus

A sudden and unexpected windfall could come your way today. However, this is unlikely to be in the form of cash because it is much more likely to be in the form of a bargain for the home. You may find just the piece of furniture you are looking for advertised on the notice board in your local supermarket. You could find a bike for the kids or, possibly a useful tool or a gardening implement at just the right price.

Sunday, 28th September
Mars into Sagittarius

Mars moves into your solar house of finance and income from today and draws your attention to urgent matters that should have been dealt with long ago. If you've let your economic realities slide then now's the time to rectify the situation before the expense becomes unbearable. You can focus an abundance of energy towards increasing your income now. Unnecessary expenditures will be reviewed and some much-needed economies made. Swift action is your forte.

Monday, 29th September
Void Moon

This is one of those days when none of the planets is making any worthwhile kind of aspect to any other planet. Even the Moon is 'void of course', which means that it is not making any significant aspects. On such a day, avoid starting anything new and don't set out to do anything important. Do what needs to be done and take some time off for a rest.

Tuesday, 30th September
Mercury trine Neptune

When Mercury, planet of the mind, and the confusing Neptune fall into aspect there are always muddles. Talking at crossed purposes is a common feature today, as you and your friends encounter misunderstandings galore. If you have got anything to say other than idle chit chat, then make sure that your meaning is crystal clear. You'll find that most problems occur because no one has all the facts.

October at a Glance

LOVE	♥	♥	♥	♥	
WORK	★	★	★	★	
MONEY	$	$	$	$	$
FITNESS	ⓦ	ⓦ			
LUCK	♘				

Wednesday, 1st October
New Moon

The world of romance is especially attractive on a day when your dreams and fantasies take over your life. The New Moon points the way to new emotional experiences in the future, but you mustn't cling to the past because of misplaced loyalty or guilt. Some people are leaving your life, but if you are honest you'd admit that they're no real loss. Follow your instincts now and your dreams may well come true.

Thursday, 2nd October
Mercury into Libra

You'll find yourself in a more introspective mood because Mercury, planet of the mind enters the most secret and inward-looking portion of your horoscope from today. This is the start of a period when you'll want to understand the inner being, or your own desires and motivations. Too much of a hectic life will prove a distraction, now so go by your instincts and seek out solitude when you feel like it.

Friday, 3rd October
Mercury sextile Mars

Your mind is going at full pelt just now and it will be extremely easy for you to find the answers to a number of problems just by thinking about them for a while. Whether what you are trying to sort out is practical, financial, emotional or spiritual, you seem to be guided by some higher power today.

Saturday, 4th October
Sun trine Jupiter

Get set to take off to foreign climes. You seem keen to get away from it all and explore a different part of the world now. You may have a secret desire to visit a particular place and if so, why not do something about it today?

Sunday, 5th October
Mercury trine Uranus

You may be expecting to go out and about today, only to find that something changes your mind and keeps you indoors instead. Take some time off to read a book or indulge yourself by watching a video or two.

Monday, 6th October
Venus sextile Neptune

Compassion flowers under the gentle influence of Venus and Neptune today. Although you aren't generally known as a forgiving sort, you will be prepared to forgive and forget now. Old hurts and offences are put in the perspective of the times they occurred, as you realise that there's no need to carry the burden of vengeance with you any longer. In fact, a more spiritual awareness helps you to come to terms with many memories that have previously haunted you.

Tuesday, 7th October
Venus into Sagittarius

Your financial state should experience a welcome boost for a few weeks as Venus, one of the planetary indicators of wealth, moves into your solar house of possessions and economic security from today. You feel that you deserve a lifestyle full of luxury now and that'll be reflected in the good taste you express when making purchases for your home. Your sense of self-worth is boosted too, which might indicate a renewed interest in high fashion.

Wednesday, 8th October
Jupiter direct

Jupiter turns to direct motion in your fourth solar house today and this will be of great benefit to those of you who are trying to buy, sell or improve your home. The same thing applies to any property or premises that you buy, sell or rent for business or even investment purposes. In short, the next few months are a good time for any kind of property dealings.

Thursday, 9th October
Neptune direct

The planet Neptune returns to direct motion today bringing an extremely subtle, yet powerful influence to bear. Slowly, you'll find your thoughts clearing. Problems that had confused you will now seem simple, and you'll wonder why you didn't see the solutions before. Even the most complex issues can now be resolved because you'll be able to apply your intuition to them. Neptune's forward motion should also help you to sort out your priorities.

Friday, 10th October
Sun opposite Saturn

You may find it hard to get along with older men today.

Father figures and authority figures will be awkward and demanding, and they may wear you out with requests to run this way and that in order to satisfy their need for power. Your own confidence level is at a low ebb and you may do or say something that you feel is foolish. Don't worry, nobody will notice – they are all to busy studying their own egos to bother too much with yours.

Saturday, 11th October
Venus conjunct Pluto

There should be quite a bit of extra money coming your way today. This may be something that you have worked for and that you expect to come in, rather than an out-of-the-blue windfall, but it is welcome for all that.

Sunday, 12th October
Venus sextile Uranus

If you were expecting a nice peaceful day at home alone, then forget it. Friends and relatives will drop in for tea, coffee, chats and sympathy all day long. It may not be what you had planned but you will enjoy it all the same.

Monday, 13th October
Sun conjunct Mercury

The Sun and Mercury move into close conjunction today, and this heightens your imagination. It is too easy to get carried away with an idea now and let baseless fears rule your life. You're quite emotional now, so when the light of reason is overwhelmed by your ego, your anxieties come to the fore. Don't be taken in by flights of fancy.

Tuesday, 14th October
Uranus direct

The large and eccentric planet, Uranus, turns to direct motion today, thereby ending a period of unpredictable events in your family circle. There have been reasons for some of your loved ones' strange behaviour, but because you didn't know what these were, it has been hard to understand their activities. Gradually all will become clear once again.

Wednesday, 15th October
Mars sextile Jupiter

You are keen to expand your horizons now, so take a look around and see how you can make your life just that little bit bigger and better than it is at present. You can take a bit of a financial gamble today if you want to, because the planets suggest that your luck is holding up quite well just now.

Thursday, 16th October
Full Moon

Something is coming to a head in relation to your work. This is not a major crisis and there is absolutely no need to flounce out of a perfectly good job, but there is a problem that should be solved before you can continue on in a happy and peaceful frame of mind. You may have to sort out what your role is and which part of the job other people should be doing, because it looks as if you are carrying too much of the load at the moment.

Friday, 17th October
Mercury square Neptune

Your mind and your heart seem to be going in two different directions today. You want to contact people, get some work done and do some serious negotiating, but your heart is set on day-dreaming. The only way to cope is to do only what needs to be done and then take some time out for drifting and dreaming.

Saturday, 18th October
Venus sextile Jupiter

Cash luck is on its way to you soon because those two most fortunate planets, Venus and Jupiter, are in a most generous mood and will bestow their financial blessings freely.

Sunday, 19th October
Mercury into Scorpio

The movement of Mercury into your own sign signals the start of a period of much clearer thinking for you. You will know where you want to go and what you want to do from now on. It will be quite easy for you to influence others with the brilliance of your ideas and you will also be able to project just the right image. However, guard against trying to crowd too much into one day.

Monday, 20th October
Sun square Neptune

Vague is the best word to describe you today! The Sun makes a negative aspect to Neptune which makes you more than a little scatter-brained. But before you start blaming others for not understanding your wishes and intentions, make sure that you explain yourself clearly. Although *you* might know what you mean, it's a bit much to ask others to become telepathic overnight.

Tuesday, 21st October
Mars trine Saturn

You'll be very decisive today. Your common sense is powerful as indeed is your capacity to carry out your decisions to a successful conclusion. You'll overwhelm any opposition with ease. If you've been under the weather, the martial aspect to Saturn is a good indicator of recovery.

Wednesday, 22nd October
Mercury square Uranus

You could be a little too blunt for comfort today since you won't be able to see any earthly reason why you should keep your opinions to yourself, no matter how controversial they might be!

Thursday, 23rd October
Sun into Scorpio

The Sun moves into your own sign today bringing with it a lifting of your spirits and a gaining of confidence all round. Your birthday will soon be here and we hope that it will be a good one for you. You may see more of your family than is usual now and there should be some socialising and partying to look forward to. Music belongs to the realm of the Sun, so indulge yourself with a musical treat soon.

Friday, 24th October
Venus trine Saturn

Some serious thought about your financial future would not go amiss today. Setting up a savings scheme of some kind into which you can make regular contributions would be a very good idea.

Saturday, 25th October
Venus conjunct Mars

Self-restraint is impossible when Venus and Mars come into close contact in your financial sector today. All those things that you strongly desire will be overwhelmingly tempting now. Gone are thoughts of budgeting and economic restriction, because you're going to indulge your taste for the finer things in life no matter what the cost.

Sunday, 26th October
Moon sextile Mercury

Prepare yourself for a party. It may not be planned, but the lunar aspect to Mercury ensures that an impromptu affair has all the makings of a splendid time. Forget your duties for now and accept any invitation that comes your way without a second thought. On the other hand, you may find your home invaded by friends determined to have a good time.

Monday, 27th October
Mercury square Jupiter

Watch out for thieves and confidence men today! Don't allow strangers into your home and, if that man on your doorstep swears that he is from the gas board or the electricity company, then quietly but politely shut the door for a moment and phone the relevant service in order to check on him. Watch your purse, lock your car, shut your back door while you are in the front watching the television. If you have an outside light at the back of your house, leave it on tonight. (If not, leave on an inside light and allow it to shine outwards.)

Tuesday, 28th October
Sun square Uranus

Expect a shock from a family member today. Your preconceptions are about to be challenged by a revelation. The important thing is to keep calm and not over-react!

Wednesday, 29th October
Moon opposite Saturn

One or both of your parents may give you cause for concern today. They may be ill or out of sorts and in need of a bit of comfort and sympathy. If you don't have parents any more, this could apply to any older friend or relative who you are close to, or for whom you feel responsible.

Thursday, 30th October
Moon square Neptune

Though soft-hearted, your good nature could be taken advantage of today. Sob stories abound, and though you are aware that some people are far worse off than you, it wouldn't do to put yourself out too much for someone who will turn out to be a sponger.

Friday, 31st October
New Moon

There's a New Moon today. This is a powerfully positive influence that encourages you to make a new start. Personal opportunities are about to change your life! You must be prepared to leave the past behind to embark on a brand new course. Decide what you want, because you'll be your own best guide now.

November at a Glance

LOVE	♥	♥	♥		
WORK	★	★	★	★	
MONEY	$	$	$	$	
FITNESS	〰	〰	〰	〰	〰
LUCK	♘	♘	♘	♘	♘

Saturday, 1st November
Moon conjunct Mercury

You are likely to be the starring act today wherever you happen to be. At work, your ideas will shine and at home, your scintillating wit will impress your family and friends. You will be so sharp that you are in danger of cutting yourself on your own tongue!

Sunday, 2nd November
Moon sextile Uranus

You will have a very clever money-making idea today and, whether this makes you a fortune or simply brings in a small but useful sum, it will be worthwhile. You could stumble across something that looks like a broken piece of junk in a jumble sale or a car boot sale, only to find on closer inspection that it is either something quirky but useful in your present circumstances, or even that it is highly valuable.

Monday, 3rd November
Moon trine Saturn

Hard work is the order of the day and that's just the way you'll like it. You're in the mood to get things done and won't let petty details get in your way. Others had better watch out because you won't be in the mood for any shirking.

Tuesday, 4th November
Sun square Jupiter

There seems to be some kind of practical problem in your home just now. Perhaps you need to buy furniture or carpets for a child's bedroom. Whatever this is, try to wait for a day or two before plunging into expense or debt, however tempting this may seem to be. This is because there are better deals to be had and better times in which to do this coming your way soon.

Wednesday, 5th November
Venus into Capricorn

The movement of the planet Venus into the area of communication and travel shows that you're starting an extremely social period. Intellectual discourse will be as alluring as physical attraction now so you'll enjoy many varied conversations. You have a natural ability to put your point of view across with charm and persuasion. Keep an open mind though, because you can learn such a lot at this time.

Thursday, 6th November
Moon conjunct Neptune

A soft and gentle atmosphere is forecast today as the Moon meets up with sensitive Neptune. Read a good book or visit an art gallery to make the most out of Neptune's refined rays.

Friday, 7th November
Mercury into Sagittarius

All the planets seem to be restless just now since Mercury changes sign today. At least you can get your mind into gear concerning the state of your finances now. Tasks you've been putting off like cancelling useless standing orders, or ensuring you receive the most advantageous interest from your savings, will be tackled with ease now.

Saturday, 8th November
Moon square Mercury

Before you over-react or fly off the handle in any way, make sure that you've got the right end of the stick. Misunderstandings are rife today, especially when it comes to money. Of course, the same restrictions you apply to others aren't going to be applied when it comes to your pleasures, so to cap it all you're inclined to be a spendthrift. Slow down for today at least, and hide your credit cards!

Sunday, 9th November
Mars into Capricorn

Mars marches into your communications house today, so being direct, not to say forceful in speech will be a feature of the next few weeks. If you've got something to say then there's no power in heaven or earth that's going to prevent you from saying it! If talking to a friend or relative has been like walking on eggshells, you'll make it clear that you aren't going to pussyfoot around sensitive topics any more. Be prepared for some heated words to clear the air.

Monday, 10th November
Mercury conjunct Pluto

Don't allow others to talk you into doing something that you really feel is wrong for you. If you can avoid lending anything today, then do so. On the other hand, guard against manipulating others for your own ends now. If something needs to be changed, you have the courage to do it.

Tuesday, 11th November
Mercury sextile Uranus

Good news connected with money is due today, and you could find that you will be very much better off no matter how unlikely that prospect seems. A relative too may have a windfall.

Wednesday, 12th November
Moon square Neptune

It's a worrying sort of day under the influence of the Moon

and Neptune. Everything seems so black and depressing as you look to the future with a pessimistic frame of mind. You are really concerned about your own abilities. Whether you are up to taking on the challenges that await you. Try to be more realistic. The picture isn't as grim as you believe. If you take an unbiased look at your life, you'll see that there's plenty to be hopeful about.

Thursday, 13th November
Moon trine Venus

Any problems that have been plaguing your personal relationships will melt away today. They may return at another time but for now, peace and quiet will reign. A female friend will do much to calm you down and to help you to regain your sense of humour and proportion.

Friday, 14th November
Full Moon

The Full Moon shines in the area of close relationships today. Since it is a stress indicator, you'd be wise to build some bridges within a close partnership now, either that or be content to let an emotional link drift . . . possibly away! Your understanding and tolerance will be the key to relationship success.

Saturday, 15th November
Jupiter sextile Saturn

You should get the glint of light at the end of the tunnel today. Hard work is now showing signs of paying off and you'll be glad that you put so much time and effort into a domestic project in the past.

Sunday, 16th November
Mercury trine Saturn

The news from your place of work is rather good today.

There may be a bit more money in the offing for you, or it may be that your status as a worker is about to rise. You may be offered some extra clerical help or someone may buy you a machine that makes your work considerably easier to do.

Monday, 17th November
Mercury sextile Jupiter

You are in a mood of expectancy and you are probably right to feel this way. You may have a pet project on the boil or you could be looking forward to a pleasant future event. All this may be just over the horizon or way off in the distant future, but either way it's nice to have something to look forward to. Better still, the chances are that the event, when it does happen, will come up to your expectations.

Tuesday, 18th November
Uranus sextile Pluto

Today's sextile aspect between Uranus and Pluto is not a short-term event. This planetary aspect will change your life – especially your home life – for the better, but it will take months before the transformation is complete.

Wednesday, 19th November
Sun sextile Neptune

Neighbourhood or family problems that have totally confused those around you will prove no challenge to your astute perceptions now. You may have to be rather cunning to get them to listen to your point of view, but once they do it'll dawn that the answer is in their hands. Don't hesitate to exert your influence for a worthy cause. The gratitude you receive will be overwhelming.

Thursday, 20th November
Venus square Saturn

It would be easy to dismiss problems today because you're likely to be in an optimistic mood, and have a tendency to overlook your own shortcomings. The truth is not as rosy as you would like though, and you'll have to admit that there's more work to be done before you can reap the rewards.

Friday, 21st November
Moon square Sun

There could be some kind of power struggle going on today. In practical terms, this could bring you up against an authority figure or someone who thinks rather a lot of themselves. This could also make things difficult for any business dealings that you have on the go at the moment. However, on a less practical note, you may doubt your own judgement for a while.

Saturday, 22nd November
Sun into Sagittarius

Your financial prospects take an upturn from today as the Sun enters your house of money and possessions. The next month should see an improvement in your economic security, and it may be that you need to lay plans to ensure maximum profit now. Don't expect any swift returns for investments, but lay down a pattern for future growth. Sensible monetary decisions made now will pay off in a big way.

Sunday, 23rd November
Moon trine Venus

Your mood will improve greatly today and the sun will shine on all your relationships. It will be easy for you to attract members of the opposite sex or to impress others with the originality, freshness and brightness of your image. You will look and feel absolutely right and you will be able to cash in on your confident and outgoing mood by impressing those who matter.

Monday, 24th November
Moon sextile Sun

Money may be the root of all evil but it's worse still not having any! It is obvious that you are doing a lot of thinking about the state of your finances, and more importantly, the things of true value in your life today.

Tuesday, 25th November
Moon square Mars

I don't know what's got you into such an irritable mood today, but your temper is almost at boiling point. The likelihood is that the cause of concern is again money. However, you aren't going to solve a cashflow crisis by taking your anger out on people who are trying to help you out. If blame lies anywhere, it lies with you! Admit that and you'll be half-way to taking a sensible stance over financial questions. Approach the problem head-on and use that pent-up energy in a good cause.

Wednesday, 26th November
Mars square Saturn

There could be great news for you and your loved ones today, but it may be some time before you can put anything into action. If there is money on the way, you will have to wait for others to send this on to you. There could be some kind of bureaucratic foul-up which sends your sponduliks to the wrong address, or just that everything seems to be taking so much time.

Thursday, 27th November
Sun conjunct Pluto

You really should sit down and work out a sensible budget for the coming months. If you are in a relationship or a business partnership, then shared resources need to be discussed as well.

Friday, 28th November
Sun sextile Uranus

A kind of breakthrough could occur today. This may be a stroke of genius on your behalf or a really cracking idea that is put to you by a friend. The outcome could be an opportunity to increase your funds. If you are looking for a new place to live, you could stumble across just the right thing today and, what is more, this could happen in the most bizarre manner.

Saturday, 29th November
Moon conjunct Pluto

There is a definite turning point now in connection with your financial position. You have probably had enough arguments over who owns what to last you a lifetime, and now is the time to start getting this settled for good. There may be a delay or a problem in connection with a contract or an agreement, but something should happen now to speed up your progress.

Sunday, 30th November
New Moon

Today's New Moon shows that your financial affairs have reached a point where you have to make a decision. Do you carry on in the old, and rather dreary ways of making and spending your cash, or will you look at the realities and make sensible decisions? This isn't a time to retreat into dreamland. Look at your monetary state carefully now.

December at a Glance

LOVE	♥	♥			
WORK	★	★	★		
MONEY	$	$	$	$	
FITNESS	◓	◓	◓	◓	◓
LUCK	☡	☡	☡	☡	☡

Monday, 1st December
Moon conjunct Mercury

You may think that you're putting up a good front, revealing nothing and letting your rational approach to all problems govern the day. But it just goes to show how mistaken you can be. In fact, your emotions are very much in evidence influencing many of your decisions. I'm not saying that this is wrong, but just be aware that you aren't the calculating machine you consider yourself to be.

Tuesday, 2nd December
Moon square Saturn

Your anxiety levels will be high today, possibly because you are worried about events at work or have a minor health problem that is getting you down. Try to be as positive as possible and take it easy!

Wednesday, 3rd December
Moon conjunct Venus

What a wonderful day to meet your pals and have a good old gossip. Women friends will have all kinds of fascinating news to impart and some of these snippets could be extremely handy for you to know. This is also a great day to go job hunting, especially if your work is in the building, farming or catering industries. Today is also great for traditionally feminine pursuits such as cooking or flower arranging.

Thursday, 4th December
Sun trine Saturn

Financial and work problems ease today as the sun breaks through the clouds of gloom that have afflicted you. Difficulties will now be easier to solve and you will gain a renewed self-confidence.

Friday, 5th December
Moon conjunct Jupiter

You could be on the move in some way now. Some of you may move house in the near future, while others may buy a second home, a timeshare or even a caravan trailer to travel around in. You may decide to get away and live in someone else's house for change.

Saturday, 6th December
Venus conjunct Neptune

Gentle pursuits away from all pressure is your idea of heaven today. Venus unites with Neptune on a day when harmony should reign supreme. Avoid all conflicts now, for your sensitivities are rather exposed and you're far too vulnerable to be left in the company of rough or ill-mannered people. You won't be in any mood for hard work either, so a day of good food, pleasing music and quiet contemplation will suit you down to the ground.

Sunday, 7th December
Mercury retrograde

Whenever Mercury moves into retrograde motion, you can

expect a short period of muddles and misunderstandings. This is not a good time to try to sort out arguments or differences in business if you can avoid it. Leave everyone to simmer down for a while and, if the situation still needs a few words in two or three weeks' time, have a go at it then when you're ready.

Monday, 8th December
Moon square Mercury

You may feel slightly irritated today and it may be hard to get any sense out of anyone. You could be a bit under the weather and something unpleasant such as a cold or a visit to the dentist may spoil your day. Everything to do with work will be awkward and irritating, and it will be hard to get new projects off the ground. Neighbours and colleagues could get on your nerves and even the cat may be too demanding! All in all, a bit of a duff day.

Tuesday, 9th December
Sun sextile Jupiter

This is a good time to look into anything to do with property or premises. You can start to look for a new home or you may decide to improve the property you are already living in. Business premises of some kind may also figure in your life now and, if you need to find these, the right ones seem to be just around the corner.

Wednesday, 10th December
Moon trine Mercury

If you're the type that keeps your thoughts to yourself, then spare a thought for your partner who could be wondering what's going on in that brain of yours. Today's stars give you the chance to tell all and explain your motivations and desires. Don't be afraid of rejection or laughter, because you'll find that someone special is very much in tune with your thoughts.

Thursday, 11th December
Moon square Jupiter

Your horizons seem to be shrinking at the moment. There are many possible reasons for this kind of situation and one instance may be temporary limitations due to a health problem, or that you have to look after either an older or a younger person in the family for a while. Either way, you won't be able to stray very far at the moment.

Friday, 12th December
Venus into Aquarius

Venus moves into your solar area of home life and domestic affairs from today, ushering a period when the sanctity of your home is the most important thing in the world to you. This is an excellent time to put an end to an old feud that's been harming the unity of your family. Don't be afraid to make the first move towards peace, as no one will think the worse of you. In fact, your offer of friendship will enhance your reputation. Venus also inspires your taste, so many will wish to refurbish your abode to the highest standards in the run up to Christmas.

Saturday, 13th December
Mercury into Sagittarius

Mercury's timely entry into your financial sector should be a great help to your situation. Your mind will now be clear and you can see all issues from a logical standpoint. Now you'll be able to budget sensibly, pay off outstanding debts and generally make sense of your cashflow. The shrewdness that Mercury brings to bear on your economic life will enable you to control income and expenditure.

Sunday, 14th December
Full Moon

The Full Moon brings to the surface intense feelings that you have buried away in some vault of memory. You'll be forced to look at yourself stripped bare of illusions now. That's not such a bad thing, because you'll realise that many of your hang-ups have been a total waste of time and should be ditched. You may have a financial worry coming to a head, so today's Full Moon encourages you to take decisive action to sort it out once and for all.

Monday, 15th December
Mars conjunct Neptune

Everything is urging you towards taking action today, so you won't be able to resist getting on the 'phone, writing letters and getting things moving. You will also be keen to jump into whatever vehicle you have at your disposal and rush around the neighbourhood. All this would be great, but for the fact that Neptune will make it hard for you to concentrate properly, so take care while driving and with what you say on the 'phone or, more importantly perhaps, on paper.

Tuesday, 16th December
Saturn direct

Saturn is turning to direct motion in the area of your chart that is devoted to duties and employment and also health. This suggests that, if you have been struggling to get though your working days, things should go more quickly and easily from now on. You will start to receive the recognition for the efforts that you have been making and you may begin to feel less fatigued with it all.

Wednesday, 17th December
Sun conjunct Mercury

This is an excellent day on which to pull off a really spectacular deal, so if you feel like wheeling and dealing in the big leagues, then do so today! Even if you are only looking around for something for yourself or your family, you should be able to find just what you want now. This is also a good time to buy, sell or repair a vehicle.

Thursday, 18th December
Mars into Aquarius

Your energies will be directed to your home and the area around it, so you may spend time working around your home today. If the dishes are piling up in the kitchen get down to washing them up, and if you haven't a clean shirt or a pair of socks to match, then get around to doing the washing now. Mars in the domestic area of your life over the next few weeks could bring a rash of plumbers, builders and all kinds of other domestic work people your way.

Friday, 19th December
Moon square Pluto

A friend is likely to put you into an embarrassing situation today because they may ask for a loan, and you may not want to give it to them. If the friend needs money, then consider a small sum that you could give them without really missing it. Don't lend, give; and then forget about it. If a friend wants to borrow an item that belongs to you, then weigh up if you are likely to get this back and then decide if you need your friend or your goods the most.

Saturday, 20th December
Mercury sextile Jupiter

Jonathan and Sasha don't advocate gambling as a rule, but a small and insignificant wager today could bring results.

For strange astrological reasons, we suggest that you try your hand at a little bingo, lotto or housey-housey today and leave the gee-gees alone. Although a bet on a horse with a name that includes the words 'house' or 'home' may work. Don't blame us if you lose your shirt!

Sunday, 21st December
Sun into Capricorn

Your curiosity will be massively stimulated from today as the Sun enters the area of learning and communication ushering in the Winter Solstice. Other people's business suddenly becomes your own now. That's not to say that you turn into a busybody overnight, it's just that many will turn to you for some guidance. Affairs in the lives of your brothers, sisters and neighbours have extra importance now. Short journeys too are well starred for one month.

Monday, 22nd December
Venus conjunct Mars

You should be able to enjoy the company of older members of the family now, especially mother figures. You may find that a maternal person is exceptionally helpful now, and this will lead to a better understanding within your family. This is a wonderful time for all those who are looking for somewhere to live or who are seeking business premises. If you are getting together with someone in order to make a first home together, this is especially well starred.

Tuesday, 23rd December
Moon trine Jupiter

A happy domestic atmosphere prevails today and you will be content just to sit quietly in your own space while your family do their own thing . . . as long as they are happy to leave you in peace.

Wednesday, 24th December
Moon sextile Sun

A reunion with a brother, sister, or other member of your family that happens to be of the same generation as you will be a marvellous plus factor on this Christmas Eve. You'll get the chance to have a long talk and catch up on all the gossip.

Thursday, 25th December
Moon square Jupiter

Too much of a good thing often turns sour, and this is particularly true when you are invaded by all and sundry this Christmas Day. Everyone wants to be social and to have fun, except you. You'd much rather have some peace and quiet!

Friday, 26th December
Venus retrograde

Family disagreements which were swept under the carpet long ago may surface again as Venus goes into retrograde motion. A female relative could be troublesome and will need careful handling.

Saturday, 27th December
Mercury direct

If the last few weeks have seen messages going astray, endless wrong numbers and posted cheques that never arrive, the planet Mercury's to blame. Fortunately the tiny planet resumes a direct course today which should improve the situation considerably. If any misunderstandings have crept in recently, you can now put matters right with little trouble at all.

Sunday, 28th December
Mars conjunct Uranus

Harsh words and rebellious attitudes are to be expected in your family circle today. The conjunction of aggressive Mars with unpredictable Uranus could open up a can of worms. It may not actually be serious, but it will certainly be loud.

Monday, 29th December
New Moon

The New Moon shows a change in your way of thinking. In many ways you'll know that it's time to move on. Perhaps you'll find yourself in a new company, a new home or among a new circle of friends in the near future. Opinions are set to change as you are influenced by more stimulating people. Perhaps you'll consider taking up an educational course of some kind.

Tuesday, 30th December
Moon conjunct Neptune

A gentle day in which you should give yourself over to the finer things in life. Read a good book, or expand your knowledge or aesthetic tastes. Make the most of this Neptunian influence by listening to music or visiting an art gallery or museum.

Wednesday, 31st December
Moon conjunct Venus

This last day of the year should be a good time for your family and your home life. Relatives may pop in with offers of help and useful gifts. Any family get-together will be extremely successful. This is a good time to buy something beautiful or even valuable for your home, or to arrange for refurbishment. This is a good day to pick up collectors' items such as antiques, objects d'art or other good things for the home.

ASTROLOGY FOR LOVERS

The Classic Guide to Love and Relationships

Liz Greene

This comprehensive guide to life, relationships and lovers provides an accessible and readable introduction to astrology.

Liz Greene, from her standpoint as trained psychotherapist and astrologer, explains the principles of astrology, debunks popular myths and shows how an understanding of the subject helps in forming lasting relationships.

Included are:

- the personality of each astrological sign
- an explanation of the shadow side
- the difference between the male and female of each sign
- how each sign behaves in love and out of love
- a quick guide to working out your ascendant sign.

UNDERSTANDING ASTROLOGY

A Practical Guide to the Stars

Sasha Fenton

Understanding Astrology provides a concise introduction to this ancient art, showing how it can be used to assess a person's character.

This book takes you beyond the person's 'sun sign' and shows you how to read birth charts. Every element of the horoscope is discussed in simple summaries, along with instructions on how to construct a chart for yourself.

Complete with sample birth charts and astrological tables, this book serves as an ideal starting point for anyone taking their first steps in the fascinating study of astrology.